Culture, Clichés, and Conversations

Other Books By the Author

Common Threads: Investigating and Solving School Discipline (2013)

The Hidden Principalship: A Practical Handbook for New and Experienced Principals (2013)

The Hidden Teacher: Not Only Surviving the System, But Thriving in It! (2014)

Culture, Clichés, and Conversations

Cultivating Relations Between Teachers and Administrators

Anthony Barber

ROWMAN & LITTLEFIELD
Lanham • Boulder • New York • London

Published by Rowman & Littlefield
A wholly owned subsidiary of The Rowman & Littlefield Publishing Group, Inc.
4501 Forbes Boulevard, Suite 200, Lanham, Maryland 20706
www.rowman.com

16 Carlisle Street, London W1D 3BT, United Kingdom

British Library Cataloguing in Publication Information Available

Library of Congress Cataloging-in-Publication Data

Barber, Anthony
Culture, cliches, and conversations : cultivating relations between teachers and administrators /
Anthony Barber.
pages cm.
Includes bibliographical references.
ISBN 978-1-4758-0898-8 (cloth : alk. paper) — ISBN 978-1-4758-0899-5 (pbk. : alk. paper) —
ISBN 978-1-4758-0900-8 (ebook)
1. School management and organization—United States. 2. School environment—United States. 3.
Teacher-administrator relationships—United States. 4. Teachers—United States—Attitudes. 5.
School principals—United States—Attitudes. I. Title.
LB2805.B273 2014
371.2—dc23
2014010631

Printed in the United States of America

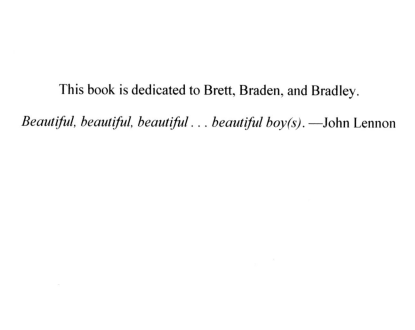

This book is dedicated to Brett, Braden, and Bradley.

Beautiful, beautiful, beautiful . . . beautiful boy(s). —John Lennon

Contents

Disclaimer

This text is offered solely as a guide and potential resource for educators who live and work in a constantly changing and dynamic environment. It is not intended to be and indeed is not an all-encompassing work that addresses each and every potential situation or issue that is or may be encountered in the realm of education. It does not provide a step-by-step guaranteed manual for success via wooden application of the concepts, ideas, and suggestions presented herein. Instead, this is a rendering and distillation of information crafted by an educator that may be of use to other educators. The application of that information is wholly dependent on the innumerable facts and circumstances and other intangible components that are part and parcel of each individual challenge or opportunity that may be presented in any individual situation.

Foreword

> If you place two living hearts cells from two different people in a Petri dish, they will, in time, find and maintain a third and common beat.
> —Molly Vass

Hidden in our biology is the secret power of relationships. The essence of life is to join together. Relationship is a natural, human state. Communication is what we are designed for, to maintain our natural state of relating to each other. It does not matter how different we are or how different our jobs are. Inside, we all search for connection. We yearn to beat in unison with each other.

In his book, *Culture, Clichés, and Conversations: Cultivating Relations Between Teachers and Administrators*, Tony Barber reminds us how essential relationships are to everything. The courage to be authentic and vulnerable and seek out opportunities to have courageous conversations is the essence of Tony's work. He moves us beyond cliché and brings us practical wisdom for developing successful conversations and successful school systems. Each chapter offers advice for both the teacher and the administrator. He focuses on balance, teamwork, and leadership. His work encourages us to go deeper in the discovery of our authentic selves and to dare greatly in discovering our truth and the truth of those with whom we are in dialogue. He humbly asks us to build our character and reduce our ego.

This should be required reading for all current and would-be administrators and teachers. It reminds us that leadership is not about accolades but humble, authentic, and honest service. I would also recommend this work to all educators who seek clear communication, deeper dialogue, and the reward of an authentic life.

Thom Stecher
Thom Stecher & Associates
thom@thomstecher.com

Preface

Relationships are at the heart of any organization. Positive ones breed successful outcomes; negative ones not so much. And in schools, the need for healthy relationships is paramount. However, far too often we find connections between administrators and teachers to be strained at best. But why?

Noam Chomsky is one of the world's most famous linguists. His work with language development, specifically the Cartesian Linguistics, discusses the nature of language as it relates to the differences that exist between human beings and animals. Arguably, one of the prime factors that separate us from the brute is our ability to limit restrictions in our thinking and language.[1]

Yet, despite this theory and research, there appears to be a wall that exists between administrator and teacher relationships, specifically when it comes to our communications with one another. Unfortunately, when we take into account Chomsky's work, we can begin to notice that this barrier is *agreed upon*, in that we are capable of greater conversations with one another, but are choosing not to have them.

Peel the onion and soon the core will present itself—*teachers and administrators rarely talk freely*. Although we pride ourselves on being advanced communicators, we often allow clichés to monopolize our discussion, which in turn create a counterculture, one that thwarts building viable contacts. Furthermore, negative discourse creates mistrust and dissention. When we engage in conversation, but know in our hearts that what we are saying is not necessarily the truth, we willingly accept bogus interactions. Unfortunately, these faulty exchanges set the stage for the next one, and the next one, and the next one, thus building a habitual pattern of relationship IOUs.

Among the teacher-observation models and data-driven everythings, perhaps a precursor is needed. Schools are a people business; without breeding sustainable relationships between administrators and teachers, student achievement will never reach its zenith. In realizing that education is power, we must look to identify the nuisances that hinder our actions to become whole. We must foster a deeper commitment in understanding each other's position within the system and among ourselves.

Admittedly, I have used all of these clichés within this text; each conveyed disenchanted dialogue and missed opportunities. Hopefully, the worth of *Culture, Clichés, and Conversations* will shine apparent by uncovering the subliminal (and not subliminal) mystic that hinders our ability to truly converse and connect.

As you contemplate the concepts in this text, please note that they are perceptions of reality. They are not meant to be the Holy Grail of educational fact. The true discovery occurs if and when we decide to talk about the issues, to engage in conversations that enter the heart of who and why we are. These are the missions born from honesty, resolve, and fearless compassion.

Ultimately, this is your journey. You may or may not agree with ideas that are discussed, and that reality is just fine. View each component as an opportunity to expand thinking, embrace the antithesis, and accept or refute what you will—that is the beauty of educational free will and a willingness to free ourselves from stagnant thinking. Happy trails!

NOTE

1. Noam Chomsky, *Cartesian Linguistics: A Chapter in the History of Rationalist Thought*, 3rd ed. (New York: Cambridge University Press, 2009).

Introduction

The text is sectioned into subjects, and chapters include concise stories, poignant discussions, and practical advice. In addition, each chapter includes real-world assistance for teachers and administrators and practical advice for both parties. Although each chapter can be explored separately, it would be helpful to review each section in order, as references are made to previous chapters.

"Setting the Stage" looks to expose the qualitative statistical assumptions and bias that accompany any research. This curt description captures the author's attitudes concerning the text and the hoped-for outcome of this exploration.

Part I is labeled "What Teachers Say about Administrators." This section identifies statements that teachers make toward administrators to define the particular situation and offer assistance for dealing with the specific circumstance from both perspectives.

Part II is labeled "What Administrators Say about Teachers." This section identifies statements that administrators make toward teachers to define the particular situation and offer assistance for dealing with the specific circumstance from both perspectives.

Part III focuses on "Clichés We All Use." Here, best-practice strategies are identified to assist teachers and administrators in dealing with these circumstances. Furthermore, practical advice is offered to assist with combating potential negative interactions.

Part IV revolves around "Practical Approaches." In this segment, the reader can explore situations and suggestions that either help or hinder building a positive culture in schools. The section offers both strategies and advice for administrators and teachers. Also included in this section are case studies. The purpose of the case study is to begin conversation by offering a similar context to discuss each issue. Case studies directly relate to each chapter.

Part V focuses on "Questions from the Field." In this part, questions are asked and addressed from different perspectives. Each question is accompanied with real-world advice on handling each potential conflict.

Part VI is titled "Looking Forward." Here, the reader will be introduced to hope's ultimate power in regard to building sustainable relationships.

Part VII summarizes the premise of the text and wishes the reader well on his or her journey into building better relationships between administrators and teachers.

Setting the Stage

So long as there are systems, there will be a need for people to govern them. Here lies the creation of hierarchy and the crux of the relationship between worker and manager, leader and those to be led.

Qualitative experts such as S. B. Merriam have stated that "qualitative researchers are interested in understanding meaning people have constructed, that is, how they make sense of their experiences."[1] Such is the quest of human interaction and the genesis for this inquiry.

As with any qualitative research, assumptions must be professed and treated to establish a more legitimate claim. In studying the topic of administrators and teachers, there are four prime assumptions that need to be revealed.

1. We are not dealing with malicious human beings.

It is assumed that people involved in the education of children would be folks who have genuine care and compassion for not only their students but other human beings as well. Although reality could dictate to the contrary, this theory is a backdrop for our discussion.

2. Both teachers and administrators desire a healthy culture.

Although the nuances of *healthy* can be debated, it is assumed that each group is willing to work toward a more collegial relationship if presented with viable strategies for attainment.

3. There is always a literal and an alternative meaning to spoken word.

Similar to adolescent flirting ("Nice day we are having"), sometimes what we say is not necessarily what we mean ("I like you"). In other words, sometimes what we say is designed to garner another response, action, or feeling. This prime assumption sets the stage for the existence and breakdown of clichés.

4. Authentic relationships are built upon trust.

The belief that a trusting relationship can prosper is the first step in this process. Trust is built with honesty; honesty requires a level of openness and a desire to participate in the process. Within this premise, relationship-building is more than a two-way street; it is a multiple intersection, paved with integrity and resolve.

BIAS

Bias is also another topic that needs to be addressed. Bias speaks to the prejudice that exists within us concerning a given topic. For this investigation, please note that the author has held the roles of teacher, principal, and currently central office employee. It is within these roles that many of the lessons have been formulated; therefore, the bias that exists consumes all stances. In simple terms, the author believes that both administrators and teachers are responsible for the development of their relationships. In finding fault with each entity, the "natural" approach for conflict resolution would come with a joint effort.

Furthermore, the various situations that have been presented are purely fictional. Although any one could resemble a myriad of daily truths within a school setting, please note that characters and conflicts are purely presented in an effort to expand each circumstance.

Also, please note that the point of view will be to defend the person being accused. For instance, in the section "What Teachers Say about Administrators," the conversation will look to refute the cliché. This type of format will be followed throughout the text.

NOTE

1. S. B. Merriam, *Qualitative Research and Case Study Application in Education* (San Francisco: Jossey-Bass, 1998).

I

What Teachers Say about Administrators

ONE

Joining the Dark Side

Movie characters sometimes supersede human expectation and parlay into the creation of legends. One such personality that transcends time is undoubtedly Darth Vader.

Born from the brain of George Lucas, Darth Vader embodied evil.[1] From his blackened cape and cavernous voice to his defiant saber and impenetrable headdress, Darth Vader was to be respected and feared. And who could forget the signature breathing? (I bet you are doing it right now.) Of all of the characters from the Star Wars series, one would be hard pressed to find a more popular, more formidable fellow than Vader.

Of all of Darth's exceptional characteristics, his most impressive was his ability to utilize the force, a powerful lifeline that controlled human reality. Those who utilized the force for good intentions were lauded as heroes; those who exploited its energy to attain prestige and power were looked upon as members of an evil entity. Such was the structure of the *Dark Side*.

Interestingly, there are places in the educational system where joining the administrative ranks can be synonymous with alignment to darkness. Such twisted terminology might be considered exaggerated; however, the simple arrangement of administrators to loathsome leadership warrants an examination.

Marion Tibbs wanted to be a principal. Having spent the last seventeen years as a fourth grade reading teacher, Marion was starting to feel a tad tired. This was not to say that his students would have ever noticed a dip in Marion's energy or performance. He still was the same positive, student-centered educator on the outside. Yet, within his mind, he wondered if there was more beyond the literacy and learning.

3

In Marion's own words, he realized that teaching students was "the most important job in the building." However, he could not help but to place himself into administrative roles. Similar to Walter Mitty, Marion dreamed of handling difficult parent situations and giving the "big speech" when it came time for various ceremonies. Like Walter, no one knew his intentions. [2]

One day, he attended an informational session on administration. It seems as though the local university was offering a cohort program at his school. A year and half of study and Marion would become certified as a principal.

Finally, Marion decided to share his vision. He discussed the pros and cons with his family and after much deliberation decided to enter the program. Excited, he was anxious to share his news with his colleagues, especially Carol, his grade-level partner.

Without promoting, Marion explained the situation to Carol. He was anxious to gauge her reaction. He thought that she might be disappointed in losing him as a partner, but was hopeful that someday they could work together as a principal-teacher team. What occurred next was absolutely not anticipated.

On hearing the news, Carol became annoyed . . . really annoyed, as if someone just slapped the last piece of pencil out of her hand. "Why would you want to do that?" she bellowed as Marion sat dumbfounded. "You know what happens to principals. They change! They become someone else."

"I think it might be challenging and fun," Marion replied.

"Challenging and fun," repeated Carol. "There's nothing fun about joining the dark side."

Marion played possum, partly because he was taken aback and partly because he felt like he was losing a friend in an instant. The meeting concluded incomplete.

Over the next few weeks, Marion tried to explain his justification to Carol and others. However, his rationalisms fell on uninterested ears. As his coursework grew, his popularity diminished. Although not to his face, some of the staff even referred to him as "one of them."

Of all of the byplay between Marion and Carol, this account's summation is found in the last three words: *one of them*. How far have we fallen to define each other as opposite ends of the educational spectrum? Marion's saga germinates an entirely new level to the disconnection between teachers and administrators. However, perhaps the view of the *Dark Side* on the surface speaks to the act of treason, but beneath the surface hides our inability to verbalize the notion of systematic balance.

"The educational system, any system for that matter, holds balance between the rights of the individuals and the rights of the collective. Within this bombardment of varying perspectives comes the necessity to create a cultural standard, a scheme that all members can understand and exist within." [3] In other words, for the system to remain stable, decisions need to be made, and ultimately, someone will have to make them.

W. Feinberg and F. J. Soltis have defined school structures in their text, *School and Society*.[4] In a classroom, the system asks teachers to keep balance. To do so, many teachers take a functional approach to school culture. In other words, functional teachers subscribe to a "fair is equal" model. In considering just sheer number, one can see why teachers follow such a path so not to create imbalance or the haves and have nots.

Conversely, guidance counselors, psychologists, special education teachers, and even parents take a more conflict-theorist approach. With this philosophy, fair is not equal, as the system itself is already out of balance in favor of the haves. Conflict theorists see the system as faulty by supporting the rights of the collective over the individual. In simple terms, these folks place the needs of the child above the management of the collective.

So how does this information fit into our dilemma? Principals are often asked to balance the rights of the individuals (conflict theorists) and the rights of the collective (functionalists) by interpreting what is needed in each decision (interpretivist). However, this responsibility does come with a price. See figure 1.1.

For instance, when you dreamt of becoming a teacher, did you say to yourself, "Boy, I cannot wait to compromise; I cannot wait to share my room; I cannot wait to acquiesce to other people's ideas"? (I know I didn't.) Chances are, when we dreamed of becoming teachers, we pictured ourselves in our classroom with the students . . . by ourselves! And the constant encroachment on teacher autonomy can sometimes feel like the life force is being sucked out of us. And guess who represents the assault on our dreams? You got it . . . the principal. (This is not to say that we did not recognize the idea of management in our profession, but we saw it as a necessary *evil*.)

In addition, within a system that promotes equality (union-based), correctness reigns supreme. In other words, when dealing with so many people (teachers within a union; students within a school system) and their governance, fair becomes equal. Witness the pattern from the classroom. Of course, not every teacher is a functionalist and being a function-

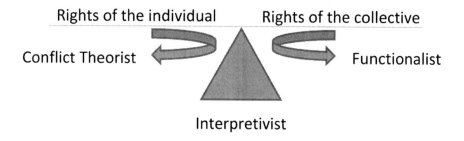

Figure 1.1.

al person is not a horrific trait. Yet the notion of someone disrupting "a fair approach to maintaining order" can be bothersome, especially when that someone "used" to be a colleague.

The notion of a boss resides in conflict with a self-governing vision. Just as Darth Vader wanted to control the rebel alliance, administrators are sometimes seen as promoters of forced compromise and blind conformity. But perhaps these thoughts stem more from our inability to discuss our fears with regard to change.

For instance, why was Carol so upset with Marion? Perhaps the real anger is caused by change and manifests itself in Marion's decision to leave his comrades, which sets the variation in motion. Maybe Carol felt that this change would alter her relationship with Marion. Certainly the openness between a teacher and administrator is different due to the privacy issues and such; however, must the change be so devastating that it destroys the relationship altogether? Maybe fear could also be prompting the feelings of hostility, as the origination of this change did not have to be made (Marion could have stayed a teacher).

Another possible idea that could be presenting itself in Carol's mind is the assumption that Marion wants to be "better" than his colleagues. In a system that dictates team (union), those who often try to surpass their colleagues are represented as selfish individuals. The latter is not an indictment on unions, but a possible explanation to the anger that arises when a person wants to be "more" than his peers.

Admittedly, there are those who enjoy being the Darth Vaders of the educational world. These folks set the table for retribution. Boss bullies obviously give a bad name to all administrators, for their alliance with ill intent and power resemble a dark approach to management. Their behavior should never be tolerated, and it is up to all of us to report their tactics to upper management.

However, for the few and far between that are mean-spirited, there are countless others who just are. Administrators are not adminis*traitors*. They are folks that have a different calling. They are no better and no worse than folks who teach for their entire career. Obviously, they hold different positions in the system, and these differences do set up different relationships, but they are not all malicious.

The key for us all is to cease the reference and perpetuation of a dark approach to management. Like it or not, systems cannot sustain without order; and accountability is not necessarily the root of all evil.

PRACTICAL ADVICE FOR TEACHERS

Don't take it personally. Although difficult, what sustains positive longevity is our ability to see actions outside of our control as possible occurrences and not plots against us. Whether Joe, Mary, or Marion is our principal, inevitably, we will have a boss. (This model is similar to the students in that they do not get to select who teaches them.) Freeing our minds from the conspiracy theory that administrators are evil beings may just alleviate a heck of a lot of stress and unnecessary worry.

See the system. The balance between the rights of the collective and the rights of the individual is made through decisions. These decisions hopefully foster stability. Becoming educated about our place within the system and the need to balance it can offer solace when decisions do not necessarily go our way. Furthermore, by understanding that systems establish outcomes, our ability to depersonalize the results can foster a better approach to building relationships with administrators.

Refrain from using the analogy. Words are power. The concealed and not-so-concealed message that stems from the Dark Side terminology is that administrators are evil. Again, someone has to sit in a position of judgment, but the intentions of that person should not be judged prior to the actions. By eliminating this verbiage from our language, we may start to build the bridge toward a better relationship. Likewise, the golden rule still works whenever we are absent of factual information. *Assume good intentions until proven otherwise; then forgive.*

PRACTICAL ADVICE FOR ADMINISTRATORS

Prove it in your actions. Nothing builds a trusting relationship like genuine actions. Talk is one thing, but actually doing what we say we are going to do assists in building capacity for honest dialogue. Likewise, your ability to explain your actions also will assist relationships. In other words, make time to chat with teachers after you have processed a referral or made a critical decision. Build in the conversation that lacks in busy schedules.

Be real; be you. Build the bridge for folks to see you as you are. Too often, the façade diminishes our ability to truly connect. Administrators are human beings; they are no better and no worse than teachers. Different jobs do not require forced prowess. Show who you are by sharing of yourself. Revealing hobbies, interests, and books you have read are all great ways to start to break down the callous condition that exists when we do not.

Share the power. You may hold the rank, but power is negotiated. Those who hoard power for self-gain usually succumb to its mismanagement. Think of your role with power as holding Jell-O in your hand—hold it too loosely, and it will slip out of your hand; hold it too tightly, and it will ooze between your gripped fingers. Build the team by being the coach who promotes it in words . . . and in actions!

Chapter 1

NOTES

1. George Lucas, *Star Wars: Episode IV—A New Hope* (San Francisco: Lucasfilm, 1977).

2. Thurber, James. *The Secret Life of Walter Mitty. The New Yorker*. NY, 1939.

3. A. Barber, *The Hidden Principalship: A Practical Guide for New and Experienced Principals* (Lanham, MD: Rowman & Littlefield, 2013).

4. W. Feinberg and F. J. Soltis, *School and Society* (New York: Teachers College Press, 1998).

TWO

That's Why You Make the Big Bucks

Linda Conrad was the principal of Ericson Central Charter and one of the busiest people she knew. In fact, most days were a blur. Be it handling a student situation, meeting with families, or observing teachers, her list of tasks seemed as vast as the Milky Way. And the staff at Ericson knew it.

Jemina Villas was a second grade teacher and had assumed the role of "mother" at Ericson. This was not to say that she was power hungry. That was certainly not the case. Jemina was simply a tremendous teacher, whose experience and innovation established her as a positive force at the school. Jemina's optimistic nature and genuine concern for folks was well documented.

On this particular Tuesday, Jemina was assisting the staff in the annual Turkey Fund preparations. The Turkey Fund was a donation drive that fed more than seventy-five families during the holidays. Many staff, students, and community members participated in the planning, preparation, and implementation of the project. Today, the packages were being assembled.

Almost everyone involved with the project felt a special bond that accompanied the season of giving. Almost everyone. Linda had yet to make it into the cafeteria, the place where the food was being organized. She was busy finishing up the bell schedule for next week's assembly program. Needing a bit of information from the cafeteria workers to complete the agenda, she managed to pop her head into the space long enough to thank everyone for their support. As she darted past Jemina, their eyes met. Linda shook her head and lifted her shoulders as if to say, "I'm crazy busy today."

Jemina politely smiled and stated, "Guess that's why you make the big bucks."

Linda's half nod told the story.

"That's why you make the big bucks" has to be one of the most popular clichés in the history of manager-worker relationships. No single cliché is more powerful in creating a counterculture in schools today than this one. And the reason has to do with its multiple meanings.

Obviously, we can all understand the literal reference to salary differential. Assumedly, administrators earn more money than teachers. This "truth" does not hold water when we compare hours worked with actual salary for some of the more veteran teachers, but the point serves. In school systems today, administrators (most times) make more money than teachers, and everybody knows it. However, aside from the salary differential, the real damage of this adage resides in the nonliteral connotation and its intent.

First, this cliché separates the user from the target as it defines the traditional distance between worker and manager. When folks make this statement, sometimes their intent is to let the administrator know that these types of specific tasks are part of being an administrator. In other words, when someone signs up to be the boss (and leaves the security and salary of teaching), one has to expect to have days like this—a not-so-subtle reference to joining the dark side or selling out.

Just as destructive, the next implication of this cliché deflects the sense of team that could permeate in this relationship. Think about it. Very rarely do folks exist or even desire to exist in isolation, especially with educators. This does not mean that we do not crave autonomy when it comes to power decisions with curriculum, instruction, assessment, etc. We do, but just as a waitress in a busy restaurant, when you are "in the weeds," it sure would be nice if someone could pick up a table or two. ("In the weeds" is an eatery term that means all of your assigned tables have been seated, and the patrons all desire your attention at once.)

Too often, administrators and teachers notice one another in the weeds, but fail to break down the habitual wall between us that may keep us safe, but also keep us apart. We allow the cliché to cloak our insecurity toward one another. (We talk, but we do not communicate.)

The culpability for such non-actions exists in both parties. As administrators, we need to hear this cliché and address its significance. We should not allow it to stop conversations but to start them. We must see the use of such a statement as a clue to our relationship with the human beings in our building. For instance, if Linda is so busy on a daily basis, how come no one seems to offer assistance to her? Now, perhaps she is a control freak. Certainly, this could be the case. But maybe the staff does not feel comfortable with their relations with Linda. By using the platitude, they avoid the entanglement of commitment. (If one refuses to tag someone, he or she does not have to play tag.)

In addition, Linda should recognize the need to be with the people during such a social, goodwill event. To place a task (the schedule) over the human beings, especially when the work is a week away, sends a terrible message to folks who look to the leader to be a compassionate being. Although busy, Linda needed to see the error in her ways.

Likewise, Jemina could have assisted with this dilemma. What if instead of saying, "That's why you make the big bucks," Jemina said, "Can I help you with something?" This more positive response could have made all the difference with Linda and the situation. *Remember, folks want to feel they are not alone—even administrators.* We may have different responsibilities, different tasks, but we all are human beings, and the desire to connect lives within us all.

The "big bucks" do not exist in educational settings in a manner that should separate us. We must solidify our relationship status by placing the human beings above tasks. Just as the food from the Turkey Fund will nourish needy families, conversations and the avoidance of clichés will feed our necessity to truly connect.

PRACTICAL ADVICE FOR TEACHERS

Extend the Golden Rule. Assuming good intentions is one of the keys to a healthy, positive career. When witnessing a colleague in the weeds, fostering a genuine, cooperative approach will go a long way in developing continued relationships. Whether taken or not, even the offer of assistance demonstrates a team approach and can help to build a more solid bond.

Let it be known. If for some reason you do not feel secure to lend a hand to your administrator, perhaps it is time to chat. Constantly wondering or worrying about the lack of a connection is not a healthy state of mind. Now, some may think it is hazardous to speak the truth to the boss, especially when one will be relaying news that could be perceived as negative. However, residing in silence and the stress that goes with it can be crippling. Instead of triangulating your fears with colleagues, go to the source.

Spread the word. If you happen to have a positive relationship with your administrator, letting folks know she is a good person will go a long way in building a better climate and culture. Simply stated, in buildings where people are not worried about their boss, morale goes up! The more we can defeat the use of the cliché, the more we can extend affirmation without attitudes. When things are not going well, people tend to let it be known. Use the same energy to promote the positive, and the results will follow.

PRACTICAL ADVICE FOR ADMINISTRATORS

If you need help, ask. People usually do not supply much empathy to those that continually complain they have "so much to do." As the principal, you probably could assign folks to achieve the desired tasks that need attention; however, the more positive position is to ask for help with a genuine approach. One person cannot do this job by him- or herself. By building capacity for teacher-leaders, administrators can and do witness a metamorphosis of positive energy.

Share your calendar. One of the best strategies to build an understanding for your tasks is to share your calendar. Remember, some will question your day-to-day activities because it is easy to witness a teacher teaching, but much more difficult to see a principal "principaling." In office or team-leader meetings, share your week's goals. Just this little insight into your world may be enough for someone to change their perspective. Now, be sure not to position your job as more important or more stressful than the teachers'. Crybabies get tissues; leaders get help.

People first. When we place tasks over people, we lose. Just as a farmer attends to the flock prior to the fields, leaders should focus their efforts on people first. If a teacher put her subject in front of the needs of the students, how would you feel? Do not make the same mistake in a different venue. Your tasks will still be there after you have dedicated time to nurturing the needs of the staff.

Quick Think

Hope is not a chore of the mind, but a choice of the heart. Choose wisely.

THREE

They're Incompetent!

When soliciting some friendly advice about becoming an administrator, a very wise and genuine principal once said, "The more you climb the leadership ladder, the more your rear end will show and to more people."

Although not the most eloquent manner in which to describe the role of management, the pictorial serves the purpose. As the leader, the spotlight is always on you. In realizing this reality, many leaders pride themselves on knowing. Master schedules, budgets, and so on, administrators are asked to become experts of certain aspects of the job to provide a consistent structure to accomplishing tasks. But are they truly ever an expert?

If we consider the formal education process, many members of management teams may have higher degrees in school administration and leadership classes, but very few have multiple degrees in subject-specific genres. For example, it is not that uncommon to have a principal who may have been an English teacher and earned his degrees in English and leadership. Such may be the case for math and science folks as well. However, it is a rarity to locate an educational leader with all three degrees and the teaching experience to go along with it.

As folks ascend the rungs of management, the notion that one will not be as technically competent in each area of the job is apparent; however, without realizing the need to foster a team approach to the work and explain the premise behind the approach, administrators sometimes appear to be devilish delegators (less technical) or control enthusiasts (more technical). By understanding that the focus must widen as we ascend in district positions, both administrators and teachers can (at the very least) realize their role in a system that supports theory and practice. But this goal is easier said than accomplished. For the sake of this topic, let us try

15

to separate and define the variation between delegators and control enthusiasts.

THE TECHNICAL EXPERT

Technical expertise demonstrates a certain mastery level of the topic. Folks with technical knowledge oftentimes present as people who may have the correct answers, for they tend to portray their points from a position of defined power. In simple terms, they know the subject and can speak to specific examples within the framework of teaching. For instance, a person who was a successful reading specialist for two decades turned principal might be able to give his opinion on shared reading with more technical expertise than, say, a principal who was an art teacher. This is not to say that an art teacher does not understand or is unable to define and implement shared reading tenets; however, the practical, personal examples may lend themselves to a more learned knowledge basis and, therefore, could carry more technical clout.

The Benefits of the Technical Expert as Administrator

One of the benefits of the technical expert administrator is their willingness to be involved in the tasks at a grassroots level. These folks are usually members of small task forces and shared committee meetings when discussions and decisions are commencing. Another benefit is the ability to utilize them as a practical resource in the process. Having a person that has "done the job" and experienced the pitfalls of specific duties can and does provide support to folks seeking ideas and assistance.

The Costs of the Technical Expert as Administrator

The obvious cost of the technical expert is his unwillingness to compromise. Since this person has practical experiences with the topic, sometimes he will position his viewpoint as gospel, in that, "I have done your job, and as the principal, I know what is best." Certainly, it is easy to step aside with the control freaks, but that is not always possible when the ultimate outcomes for achievement rest at your door.

Likewise, the technical expert lacks perspective. Oftentimes, they view the job today exactly the way it was when they were teaching. These folks sometimes forget to ask the important questions or realize that the landscape has shifted, which in turn causes stress to folks who may understand and appreciate the knowledge, but become frustrated by their inability to apply it to today's standards.

THE TECHNICAL NOVICE—THE DELEGATOR

Just as there are administrators who have an abundance of technical expertise within a given subject, there are those who simply do not have those degrees or experiences to make similar claims. Often self-coined as "visionaries," these folks lack the depth of knowledge that would position them as valuable contributors in practical planning sessions. Therefore, these supervisors sometimes find their worth in establishing the creation of ideas, but then know enough to pass the baton to others who can finish the race.

The Benefits of the Administrative Delegator

The obvious benefit of having an administrator who delegates is the increased autonomy. Rarely does a technical novice try to intercept the details of an action, for most times they are savvy enough to know their interference would hurt the project and, ultimately, disclose their lack of knowledge. As Abraham Lincoln once stated, "Better to remain silent and be thought a fool than to speak out and remove all doubt."

Another benefit to the technical novice is his reliance on the worker. In knowing that the boss cannot complete the task, the worker's stature can sometimes ascend. Obviously, the boss, especially in the private sector, could simply hire new workers; however, that reality is not as likely in schools. (Again, remember that we are starting with an assumption that these are good people.) The point here is that the administrative delegator needs help and hopefully appreciates it immensely.

The Costs of the Administrative Delegator

On the surface, this type of person can be a very good-natured individual with pristine intentions; however, oftentimes, these folks are seen as pretentious, especially if they lack a sincere gratitude for those doing the actual work. Folks can sometimes become upset or even angry if they believe that the boss continually jockeys work to them without taking any responsibility.

The administrative delegator also can be seen as lazy. If the workers are constantly attending to the details of the task while the administrator "plays solitaire in his office," folks can certainly start to wonder why the boss has the position in the first place, thus leading to a feeling of incompetence. Speaking of incompetence. . . .

Like it or not, a principal can make a determination that a teacher is incompetent based on the knowledge that he/she has performed the job; however, it becomes difficult to make the claim that a boss is incompetent if the worker has never held that position. Certainly a teacher can disagree with the manner in which a principal is "doing" the job, but to claim that someone is incompetent assumes an understanding of back-ground knowledge, which simply is not present in these types of scenar-ios.

In addition, sometimes we render someone as incompetent when they fail to attend to our desires. For example, as a teacher, did you ever have an issue that you needed handled by the principal only to have it placed at the bottom of their "to do" list? This disregard for our needs, especially after time has passed, certainly can bring a bad taste to one's mouth. Yet are we dealing with incompetency or triage?

In emergency rooms, triage, or the art of determining priorities, occurs all the time. For instance, just because a young lady has torn the flesh on her knee and is bleeding does not mean that she will go in front of the elderly man with heart issues. Emergency staff makes these determina-tions all the time, and although as the parent of the young lady, you may be really upset waiting to be seen, ultimately someone has made the decision that your little girl will be okay.

As teachers, we triage as well. For instance, if a child is about to be sick and another needs a pencil to finish an assignment, certainly your attention would go to the potentially ill. However, did you ever stop and think how the child needing the pencil feels? Chances are, we assume that he will understand that one of his peers had a more pressing issue, and thus, we needed to give our attention to her first. Now, think back to your principal in relation to this type of situation.

Principals also triage, the difference is we rarely get to witness the other priorities or comprehend the manner in which they are prioritizing.

The lack of communication between principals and teachers when it comes to time and tasks creates potential distrust. We rarely have the time to secure an explanation let alone a full-blown conversation con-cerning our issue, especially if it is petite on the grand scale. *Here is where the breakdown occurs; here is where the clichés commence.*

Claiming incompetency is a cliché. We must look to define the gaps that exist in our understanding of our jobs and our positions within the system. Just as no two snowflakes are alike, what we believe to be impor-tant can be different. Without critical conversations and openness to ex-planations, we will continue to breed a lack of understanding and mis-trust.

PRACTICAL ADVICE FOR TEACHERS

Ask the questions . . . respectfully. Although it is never a good idea to "speak up to the boss," certainly you have the right to solicit informa-tion concerning your requests, needs, and so on. Schedule a time to sit down and chat with your principal. Try not to "catch her on the fly," as those conversations are rushed and usually end up in misinterpretation.

Try to understand the decision-making that goes into your principal's prioritizing. You may not agree, but you might feel better knowing that she did not ignore your request or simply not know how to respond.

Avoid the central office snub. Relationships are reciprocal. If you have an issue with a central office person, it is quite alright to schedule a time to chat with them as well. We cannot allow distance to be the indicator of relational success or failure. Pick up the phone or send a text or email, but make the contact to solicit the details. You may not be able to know everything (protective topics, legal ramifications), but at least this person will know you have an interest in the topic.

Some folks could think it is risky to chat with administrators above the head of the principal or even feel like they will be at risk of being tagged a "complainer" by central office personnel; however, there is a tactful way to initiate conversations so that they neither threaten the authority of the principal nor are perceived as challenges to the established central direction. In addition, showing an interest in the macro-directions of the district could establish a teacher as someone who has a positive passion for the future.

Gather background knowledge. If the job of a principal is something that you are unaware of, do your best to learn as much as you can. Take a class, read an article, or chat with an administrator. Try to learn as much as you can to satisfy your desire to understand. Knowledge is power; the more you know, the more readily you will be able to substitute conspiracies with facts.

PRACTICAL ADVICE FOR ADMINISTRATORS

Never stop learning. Remember, administrators should be one of the lead teachers in the building. Nothing says "I am in this with you" than to model lifelong learning. Taking classes, reading articles and journals, or continuing to expand your educational methodology will yield huge dividends. Think clubs, instructional chats, and professional-development moments are all quality ways to rededicate yourself to the craft of teaching. We may not be experts in a particular subject, but we should strive to be educated when it comes to instructional practice.

If you do not know, admit it. Nothing gets under the skin of folks like a master of fluff. Administrators that spin the web of generalizations to cover up their ineptitude on a particular subject expose themselves as imposters. If you do not know something, just say it. No one expects you to know all the answers, but we do expect you to gather information to know the possibilities. Take the hot air, blow it into a balloon, and let it go.

Delegate with dignity. You have the rank to delegate, but the manner in which you do can make or break the relationships surrounding the project. Those who simply assign one project after another build the reputation of being idle. Even if it's just the smallest of parts, you should try to own a piece of the project. Build the team by being a member.

FOUR

They've Forgotten Where They Are From

One More Thing

Megan Dawes was not the type of person to be easily frazzled. In being a third grade teacher for almost twenty-eight years, she had seen her share of trends. However, the current state assessment system was certainly not one she, or any of her colleagues, could have ever predicted.

The long and short of the system dealt with data. Oodles of it! From teacher-effectiveness scores to student growth rates, numbers were everywhere for everyone. Megan had always tried to do her very best to accommodate the mandates, but this was taxing to say the least, and what made the situation worse (in her opinion) was the blind loyalty her principal Mrs. Simone had for it.

In wanting "no stone left unturned for a child," Mrs. Simone had introduced data meetings. Not uncommon and certainly of value, teachers adjusted their team times to participate in said meetings. However, with the new state changes, Mrs. Simone felt like there should be more. She designed additional "red zone" meetings and also looked to form mini-task force recovery teams for students who were not growing in math, science, and language arts. Teachers were "asked" to join at least two teams.

Although these efforts were well intentioned, many of the staff members felt completely overwhelmed. In an effort to assist herself and her colleagues, Megan tried to have a conversation with Mrs. Simone. While polite, there was no changing Mrs. Simone's mind. And although Megan shared three different models that would make the process more streamlined for teachers, Mrs. Simone was not budging.

The discussion broke up and Megan proceeded to the parking lot. Awaiting her were several members of the staff, all of whom were intensely interested in the outcome.

"No dice," she stated, walking toward them. "She's set on this approach," Megan ended.

"It is not this approach!" one said emphatically. "It's her approach! She has forgotten where she is from again!" Silence and exhaust fumes filled the air.

In today's educational world, school personnel are being asked to do more than ever and with greater responsibility for positive results, and Megan's story is not unlike others in this brave new world of accountability. Yet often we must ask ourselves, *Is there a tipping point?* In other words, *can too much good be a bad thing?*

From the perspective of the teachers, the answer to the previous question appears obvious. No one could argue that instructional data meetings are not a "good" idea; however, when placed on top of an already-burdened schedule, this so-called "goodness" can and does present itself in negative light.

In the real world, this type of quantitative excess seems apparent. For instance, a little cream in one's coffee often supplies a quality taste to one's palate; yet seventeen cups of cream may be overdoing it. Here, too much of a good thing may be—you guessed it—bad! The question then becomes who gets to decide on this judgment.

Clearly, the principal in this situation is the final decision-maker. And although the decision was made, one has to wonder what the long-term impact will be for this new initiative. Many a "new" plan has come and gone because the implementation process was sporadic or nonexistent. Such is the outcome of the rushed decision. However, prior to the discussions about data meetings, it is clear from these conversations that an elephant exists in Megan's school.

When teachers feel that a principal has "forgotten where they are from," most times the actions of the principal are being judged with relation to extra work. Of course teachers are used to assigning homework to students, but we forget that principals can and do also assign work to teachers. In simple terms, *principals do not forget where they are from but often do exactly what they did as teachers.* The difference occurs in that the adults (teachers) are now the students of the principal, and the idea of more work is looked on as being assigned seventy-five math problems over the weekend. (Does anyone need to do seventy-five math problems in one sitting anymore? Oh, don't get me started.)

"The interactions we employ as human beings are created and reinforced by our agreement or non-agreement. In other words, we are actually agreeing to not communicate by accepting the surface talk or easy dismissed jargon. It is within the approval of this cultural norm that we diminish our ability to be fully functional as a team."[1] By accepting the cliché, "She has forgotten where she is from," these teachers have unfortunately relinquished the power by creating an impenetrable philosophy on the part of the principal. Yielding with the disagreement, they have effectively allowed the principal to escape further justification while also cementing a negative feel to the relationship.

Observably, it would not be wise to continually engage a principal in dialogue over a disagreement that has already been discussed. Revisiting Mrs. Simone's decision could be dicey, but the choice to "live with it" is still a choice that is being made and justified by a fabricated philosophy. Failure to break down the misperception cannot simply be blamed on the administrator in this situation.

And what about Mrs. Simone? She certainly does not escape fault. Principals that do not create a hierarchy of established goals with attainable actions create stress and ultimately despair to good-hearted people. There is nothing worse than wanting to do a good job and feeling overwhelmed to the point of frustration. By not having a pulse on the barometer of the staff, Mrs. Simone overvalued the tactic over the human beings. By doing so, she is now seen as another administrator turned against the profession that assisted her in attaining her new job.

"The foundation for a solid relationship resides in our commitment to develop it. Our ability to recognize the genuine value of nurturing a relationship will ultimately lead to its flourishing." [2]

When we forget to put people first, we create the imbalance to a system that so desires it on a daily basis. The necessity to work aside one another, with honesty and open communication, will go a long way in reducing the "they have forgotten where they are from" adage to a distant memory.

PRACTICAL ADVICE FOR TEACHERS

Build your case carefully. As stated previously, you are allowed to disagree with your boss. However, those meetings should be in a more private setting and involve a plan. Bring data, think systems, and present options. Those who just complain without bringing possible solutions eventually become known as negative.

Remember the system. Can a child refuse to do your work? Certainly, but then he would have to be accountable to the ramifications of that decision. Understand that teachers are sometimes asked to perform tasks that they did not originate. Do your best with what comes in front of you and look to organize your work on the priorities. Undoubtedly, you would want to place student initiatives at the top of the list. However, be sure that your urgencies are not in direct conflict with your boss's thoughts. Correct is correct, but right is negotiated.

Make the decision to be proactive. Having routine conversations with the leadership of the district can keep you informed of upcoming projects and plans. Even if you cannot always chat with the principal or a central office person, speaking with a lead teacher or curriculum head will help you stay abreast and ease the stress of being surprised by a new initiative. Furthermore, read minutes and try to stay connected to active research. Being "in the know" is so much better than being "in the no."

PRACTICAL ADVICE FOR ADMINISTRATORS

Explain your rationale. Yes, you can make decisions based on rank, but the more effective manner is to make them based on power. We make power decisions when we force ourselves to justify the choice. Blind loyalty has no direction. Being able to offer an opportunity for intellectual discussion is at the heart of transformational leadership. Plus, would you not want the same respect from your superior?

Start with the antithesis. If we do not know what we do not know, then does it not make sense to solicit information? Too often, administrators fear the conflict and look to defend their position when the conflict did not have to exist. In other words, if we start with the antithesis of our idea, and are open to honest feedback, we will effectively disarm the fight by allowing respectful disagreement. True innovation comes when conflicts are addressed, not ignored. Be confident to allow negotiations to exist in your relationships.

Utilize a leadership team. There are no omniscient leaders. Administrators can and do build powerful, positive forces by practicing shared leadership. Simply surrounding ourselves with "yes" people does not insulate us from criticism or disruption. Build the team by allowing honesty to permeate. Share your ideas; listen to theirs. Debate. Defend. Dialogue. Share the power and watch what happens!

NOTES

1. A. Barber, *The Hidden Principalship: A Practical Guide for New and Experienced Principals* (Lanham, MD: Rowman & Littlefield, 2013).
2. Ibid.

Quick Think

It's difficult to charge an enemy you cannot see with an army that's not behind you.

FIVE

What Do They Do Up There All Day?

Susan Stout was an incredible high school science teacher. An educator for more than twenty years, she had been working in the same school the entire time. She had held several positions in the organization including her current title of department chair. By all accounts, she was well respected by staff, students, and the administrators. But today, the tide had turned.

Susan was a good-hearted person. She was not much for confrontation. In fact, she detested it. Her position had never caused her a problem before, partly because she was such a good teacher; she did not have problems with students. However, her colleagues were a different story.

Susan, in being one who "did her job," always entered the hallway at the change of class. She did this because she enjoyed seeing the students, and she also did it because it was the expectation of the administration to do so. Yet, despite being told (in emails) how important it was to be in the hallway, many of her colleagues in G4 ignored the administration's request and sat heads down at their desks.

At first, Susan tried to rally the troops during her department meetings. She would remind them of their duty, and she always made it a point to thank them on the rare occasion one did venture into the hallway. But in recent times, the students were becoming more squirrelly. (Springtime tends to do that to a high school hallway.) Susan needed help.

Susan's frustration was with her colleagues, but today was different. Today, she had to break up a potential fight between two juniors. It was an unpleasant situation. As she escorted the two girls to the main office, she was met by the head secretary. She explained the situation and on learning that all three principals were "not around," she unfortunately snapped, "I am sick of this. What do they do up here all day long?" At that, Susan forged out of the office and left the girls to sit and wait for an administrator's arrival.

This scene unfortunately reflects many school offices. Although not as dramatic a finish, the angst that folks feel when dealing with confrontation, especially with children, can be agonizing. Notwithstanding the fight that occurred between the students, the critical issues are abundant. And no issue gives us more food for thought than "What do they do up here all day long?"

Teachers have long conversed in makeshift faculty rooms, in doorways to the auditorium, and in stairwells to the gymnasium. It's what we do. With so little time to actually speak to other adults, teachers have to make time no matter the location. Conversations vary, but certainly if you have been in education long enough, you have heard someone murmur these very words: "What *do* they do?" This valid inquiry holds one of the missing links to our quest for improved relationships.

At one time, most administrators were teachers. (Some have been counselors, psychologists, etc.) One of the fundamental functions of the job of a teacher is to teach. Being able to manipulate information into instructional opportunity sets apart the good from the great. Whether a person is suitable or super, the prime function is inherent—teach in such a manner so that students garner understanding.

It is within this simple premise that holds the combination to so many misunderstandings between administrators and teachers. Prime responsibilities for principals range from student achievement goals to school safety to building a sustainable positive culture. Yet somehow we forget that the essence of all of these goals is the understanding that comes with learning anew.

People sometimes assume loyalty prior to earning it. Rank, although important, does not bring with it trust in name alone. Trust is something that comes with one's evaluation of actions and words. It comes in time and is not a coerced or chance noted. Everyone has a basic understanding of what the role of the teacher is in the organization, but few actually know what administrators do.

Principals who do not take time to educate their staff on their responsibilities fail to build a trusting culture.

This is not to state that every little action must be documented and communicated; on the contrary, if administrators spent all day communicating what they did, that is all they would do. Yet the preliminary conversations about roles and responsibilities, about how the system works, and about how each member contributes to it, appear to be absent from our cognizance.

Susan was a victim of this void. Though it wasn't stated in this vignette, her thoughts about her administrators most certainly occurred prior to her outburst. Her understanding of support waned daily as she looked for assistance. Disgruntled with her colleagues, she took that ire and passed it on to another.

Teachers desire support, just as all employees do from their boss. People want to feel that if they are doing a good job and giving a solid effort, they will not be sideswiped. Susan was no different. Did she actually want her principals in her classroom day in and day out? No. But she wanted them in the hallway because she had a dilemma that she could not solve.

Should she have just confronted her colleagues again or even told on them? Should she have hinted to her principals that she would "love to see them in G4 sometime soon"? All are valid possibilities, and each one would have solved this issue. But there is a greater divide. *The breakdown exists not in any one answer, but in the fact that this staff allowed the cliché to suffice.*

The lack of conversation limits knowledge. With the lack of knowledge comes speculation and contempt. Oftentimes, teachers think to themselves, *I'm working hard; what are they doing?* This "they are never here when you need them" mentality feeds the suspicion; therefore, the need to constantly teach what administrators do must be at the forefront of open communication.

PRACTICAL ADVICE FOR TEACHERS

Use the union. One of the primary functions of a union is to assist its members with issues. Perhaps Susan could have solicited the assistance of her representatives for support, guidance, or even action. One of the healthiest practices a union can employ is member checks. If someone is not pulling their weight on the team, a quick reminder may be just the thing. Plus, union reps chat with the administration about all types of issues. This would have been an easy one.

Suggest a "how does that work" meeting. Just as administrators can institute different programs, so too can teacher-leaders make suggestions for the benefit of all. If you have an open-minded principal, having a discussion on sharing what her responsibilities entail could go a long way in building the trust between the staff. Plus, this type of format could also be helpful with other issues that arise in the school. Set the stage for more dialogue.

Be direct with your teammates. It is always an effective plan of action to be direct with your discussions. This is not to say that one needs to be nasty. Perhaps Susan's hints to her team were lost in translation. Explaining the situation in a clear mode and defining how it is making you feel might be just the trick to garner support. If not, at least you clarified your position and the situation at hand, thus doing your part to eliminate the guesswork.

PRACTICAL ADVICE FOR ADMINISTRATORS

Address people issues without email. The ability to define situations and point to ways to solve them is the trademark of great leadership. Those who hide behind email create a cowardly impression and generate a feeling of ineffectiveness from the staff. Get out of the office and go talk to people.

Explain your role. As mentioned previously, to assume everyone knows what you do is naïve. Take the lead with this issue and teach people. If you cannot give up valuable in-service time, then make it voluntary. Order a few pizzas for lunch one day and go to town. Although not all staff members will attend, the message will be heard. Build trust with trustworthy actions. Then send out the minutes.

Use a time-checker. As silly as this idea sounds, using an alarm clock to remind you to get out of the office can be very effective. There will be days when one will be landlocked to the desk. On those occasions, communicate with the staff. You do not have to share specifics. Keeping them in the loop builds confidence and understanding. You don't have to do this, but. . . .

SIX

Let's Make a Deal

The PrinciPAL

Mrs. Diamond was very angry. This was the fourth time that her student Leo Meeks was being defiant in class. She had followed the appropriate progression in terms of school district policy for classroom management (warnings, parent contacts, teacher consequences, etc.) and had come to a point where she required the assistance of the office.

Jerry Krauss was the middle school assistant principal. Since this was his twenty-sixth year in education (the last eleven as an administrator in the same building where he taught), he was familiar with the staff, the students, and the discipline code.

One of the reasons for Mrs. Diamond's lack of satisfaction had to do with Leo. She was not used to "this type of child" in her honors classes. Leo, who had transferred in from a neighboring school district, did not seem to be the typical Hillsdale child. In fact, earlier in the honors identification process, she had questioned his admittance.

The other reason for Mrs. Diamond's displeasure was directly linked to Mr. Krauss and his approach to discipline. Known to staff as the "principal," Mr. Krauss could not help the fact that he believed his primary responsibility was to teach students about their behavior, not just blindly punish them. He was often seen chatting with students about situations and his catchphrase, "Please don't make the second mistake," spoke to his wanting each child to learn from the experiences.

Unfortunately, staff members of Hillsdale Middle School saw this type of gentle trait as a sign of weakness. Many members were turned off by his "discussions" with students when the adults had already conveyed the details of the events. Although the staff realized the discipline book "could be interpreted at the

31

discretion of the principals," they believed this reality caused more of a bartering approach to management than dictation.

Mrs. Diamond was not one to let bygones go by. She scheduled a time to chat with Mr. Krauss. During the meeting, Mrs. Diamond became highly frustrated, for every time that Jerry would ask her for clarification on a particular detail, she felt as though he was holding her on trial. From "he said he was sick the other day" to "the other students did not quite hear that," Mrs. Diamond's blood pressure rose to a point of boiling. The meeting concluded soon after.

Two days later, Mrs. Diamond was returned the original referral. It read, "I gave him a stern talking to. Let me know how it goes. Mr. K." Upon reading the note, Mrs. Diamond folded the referral into tiny pieces and placed it in her desk drawer. It was the last referral she wrote the entire year. This is a true story.

Think this scenario does not play out in schools? Think again. Of all of the topics that cause the most stress on teacher-administrator relationships, student discipline has to be one of the prime contributors. Much of the reason behind its significance has to do with the absence of process and the substitution of justice with prejudice.

First, when we think about the process of school discipline, most folks will point to their school handbook. Within these pages, one can usually locate a set of guidelines for behavior along with specified consequences for said offenses. For example, it is fairly typical that a child who is late to class could receive a warning, a detention, or more depending on the frequency of the offense. Although not cemented in stone, most discipline handbooks outline undesired behaviors and rank them according to severity (level) and impact (consequence). However, do any of these guides explain the process for investigating?

Sadly, most administrators were never taught a process for investigating in schools. This void creates a divide in trust because folks cannot explain or define their process of attaining results without being personal. For example, without having the ability to utilize a methodology for investigating, administrators are left to explain the manner in which they secured the results (and judgments) based on only their actions and beliefs. What then often happens is *we begin judging the manner in which the action was addressed instead of the action itself.*

There are texts, such as *Common Threads: Investigating and Solving School Discipline*, that establish protocols for investigating, and it would be wise on the part of an administrative team to adopt a methodology to ensure a more consistent approach by eliminating bias from the process (shameless self-promotion). Yet even if no formal process exists, it is incumbent on the principals to at the very least describe the steps that are taken when securing results of an investigation. Unfortunately, most do not. But why?

Another major factor that adds to the communication breakdown is time. Teachers are busy. Administrators are busy. On rare occasions, time drifts by like butterflies bouncing in the breeze; most times, however, time blazes on like a fuel-injected Funny Car at Pocono Downs. The speed at which schools run nowadays is frightening. This lack of time erodes the basis of solid relationships—the connection.

In revisiting Mrs. Diamond's tale, a conversation did take place prior to judgment. Yet the communication during the event, although important, is difficult to explain when the investigation is not complete. The true voids occurred before this event happened and directly after the investigation ended.

First, prior to this occurrence, there were no discussions at this school concerning student management; hence, no one shared the school's philosophy or practice to the staff or school community. *The absence of this critical conversation is the genesis for misinterpretation.* For example, suppose the leadership philosophy was built through a team approach. What if administrators and staff worked collaboratively on establishing a belief system around school discipline? As part of this work, what if there were open discipline meetings, whereby teachers could actually practice processing referrals as a group to engage in discussion and understanding? Chances are this type of practice work may have assisted in not only the issue at hand but also a host of others.

The second missing conversation occurred after Mr. Krauss's investigation concluded. Although it is not easy to judge human interactions, Mr. Krauss made a huge mistake by not circling back to chat with Mrs. Diamond. Although these conversations can be rather tough, to avoid the potential conflict creates a sense of suspicion while also communicating to the staff (intentionally or unintentionally) that the administrator is anxious about talking to teachers. Even if the justification for missing conversations is due to time constraints, the hidden message conveys suspicion, leading to beliefs systems that see principals as used-car salespeople.

Student management should be built around age-appropriate rationale. Every member of the team should be aware of the school philosophy (they may not always agree with it, but should be aware). Teams that invest the time to ensure that folks understand the philosophy and process often have fewer issues when it comes to the topic of school discipline.

PRACTICAL ADVICE FOR TEACHERS

See the antithesis. No one-size-fits-all viewpoint can encompass the spectrum of human behavior. By valuing the opposite of what we believe should happen, we allow ourselves (and the principals) an opportunity to explore various solutions to the original issue. Yes, the discipline book does give us specific consequences for specific offenses, but it also states,

"The administrator has the right to interpret this handbook in the manner in which he/she sees fit." This balance is necessary to govern individuals in a collective environment. Life is not that black and white. Circumstance has its place even in the perceived exactness of a guideline.

Use Post-it notes. There will be times when you will want to write much more on a referral than "just the facts." For those occurrences, use Post-it notes or another form of communication to secure your thoughts to the administration. Obviously, a pre-meeting would be best, but if you cannot make that happen, be sure to keep the referral clean of bias by utilizing a different approach. Also, be sure not to write directly on top of the referral, as most times what you are saying on your Post-it will appear on the referral. Whoops!

An office referral signifies giving up control for the outcome of the issue. Events that occur inside our classrooms can be interpreted and solved by us, but once we write an office referral, we surrender the control of the outcome. Although we may be coming at this issue at 100 mph, we must be aware that administrators are not. This system provides a level of due process for the student while also providing support for staff. Once we turn it in, we must take a deep breath and allow the process to commence.

Besides, student behaviors change when the student decides to change them. Numbers of detentions and suspensions may work for the student who rarely gets into trouble, but for the habitual offenders, establishing a relationship and a purpose for their learning (a connection) holds more leverage in creating internal motivation to change.

PRACTICAL ADVICE FOR ADMINISTRATORS

Form a discipline committee. Like it or not, student discipline is a hot topic in every school. Take the bull by the horns and offer sessions for folks to learn about your philosophy and practice. Better yet, create a team approach to the philosophy and practice by studying age-appropriate means. Also, use processed (change the names) or practice referrals with your team. Let them try to solve an issue and assign consequences. Nothing creates empathy like exposure. Share your minutes with the entire staff. Take the time to create trust by creating learning opportunities.

Have the follow-up meeting. Making time to have that face-to-face follow-up meeting after a discipline issue has been solved will go a long way in establishing trust. Again, folks may not agree with your outcome, but the fact that you explained your rationale will gather momentum for the next occasion. As the principal, you do not "owe" the explanation, but simply acting based on your rank will ultimately build a gap between you and the staff. Think about it: if your boss made a decision above you, would you want a chance to understand it?

Use a system. Whether you use *Common Threads* or another system, the necessity to utilize one is critical. As an investigator of behavior, you are assuming the role of a qualitative researcher. The key of this practice is to eliminate bias to gather the inside perspective. We do this by taking ourselves out of the process of gathering evidence. Those who do not use a formal system run the risk of exposing their bias on the investigation, which in turn lessens the original event and places the focus on how the event (discipline issue) was handled. Do yourself a favor—use a system.

As an Aside

Did you happen to notice the manner in which Mrs. Diamond described Leo? Might this be a reason why Mr. Krauss took his time with this referral? See it all, my friends. See it all.

Quick Think

Sometimes perfect isn't always right.

SEVEN

She Has Her Favorites

Tara Marshall, a guidance counselor at Weston Elementary School, was seated in the school library with the rest of the faculty. Today, the staff was going to meet the candidates for the job of principal at Weston. Of the three finalists, two were outside applicants and one was the current assistant principal at Weston, Ms. Rose Wilmer.

The outside candidates went first. Each spoke of attending to the health, welfare, and safety of the students and staff while also remaining diligently focused on student achievement. Once their opening introductions and formal set of nine questions were answered (members of the hiring committee asked the formal questions while the staff listened and took notes), staff members were permitted to solicit clarification on answers or simply ask new inquiries. The entire process lasted about forty-five minutes per person.

Once concluded, it was Ms. Wilmer's turn. Rose had been the assistant principal for three years and prior was an administrative liaison in a neighboring district. Folks at Weston were familiar with Rose and, for the most part, were satisfied with her work. There were many at the school who hoped for Rose to be the successful applicant, as this decision would cause less stress to the system. In other words, these people thought things were going well.

There were also those who believed Weston would be better off with another leader. Tara Marshall was one of them. Expectedly, Rose gave her opening remarks and proceeded through the questions with a degree of ease. She utilized real data and obviously had a more practical connection to answers. Once she was finished, the floor opened for questions. At that instance, Tara seized the moment.

"Ms. Wilmer, if you were indeed the candidate that was selected for the job as principal of Weston, would you still keep the same favorites that you have now?" The room went numb. Shocked by the boldness of the question, some members of

the staff put their heads down while others moved closer to the edge of their seats. This was now going to be a defining moment in the hiring process.

Let us take a different approach to the question. Instead of trying to defend that administrators do not have favorites, let us start with the antithesis. What if principals did have favorites? Would it be that uncommon for a person to gravitate to people that find consensus easy or approach obstacles in a similar manner?

Please note that in starting with the opposite, we are not suggesting that playing favorites is either right or ethical; however, school systems are not unlike life systems in that they bring human beings together for a purpose. *The more common the purpose among folks, the more it stands to reason that these individuals could align (consensus-building).* The question then becomes if administrators did have favorites, what would be the rationale behind their alignment?

As teachers, we sometimes succumb to this reality in our classrooms. This is not to say that each and every child is not valued or differentiated to the degree that each needs; yet ask any teacher in confidence whether he or she has certain students that they just connect with and chances are they would say yes. Sometimes, these children are the most cooperative; other times, these students provide for great discussion, as signified by always having their hands in the air for questions. Not purposeful planning for a teacher's pet, but the "reality of reality" exists—"Darryl knows the answers; I can rely on him if need be."

It is safe to say that administrators probably do have their favorites. Now, whether or not folks can tell who these people are is the essence of a quality leader. In other words, we all have individuals that we gravitate to in life. It stands to reason that it is similar in the work environment. However, a great leader is cautious not to favor the favorite.

For example, just because a teacher really believes in the leadership and direction the administration is moving does not mean that she should become the head of every committee. Just as with teachers and students, staff members should not be able to pick out the principal's pet.

Some that have read the previews for this text have suggested that this idea is a game of semantics. Inevitably, their argument stems from the premise that one cannot help to "favor" those who are in accord with us. There have also been those who have questioned the ethics of a leader who has favorites, even if they are hidden from the masses.

It is agreed that the topic of favorites is controversial. However, in order to have the real conversations, we must be *real*. Folks that do not agree with us have their place within the system and provide a necessary balance to its survival, our thinking, and so on. Cutting these people out of the picture would be like removing the brake from a speeding vehicle. Sure, we will arrive at our destination a heck of a lot sooner, but in what manner?

We are all individuals, and we all have likes and dislikes, including people. The key is to avoid "special treatment" based on any type of bias.

As fate would have it, Ms. Wilmer cleared her throat and delivered what was one of the most powerful, most thought-provoking answers to an adult-to-adult question ever posed at Weston: "Mrs. Marshall, if you mean will I continue to gravitate toward people who are positive, people who love students and their jobs, and want to make Weston the greatest school on earth, then my answer is yes. I do plan to continue to want to work with these folks. And I am very much looking forward to others joining in." Rose continued to model this spirit for the next decade as the principal of Weston.

PRACTICAL ADVICE FOR TEACHERS

Stay positive. Although easier said than done, people usually do not want to be around negative people. If you are the Debbie Downer of the group, you must try to work your way out of this state of mind. One suggestion would be to revisit your passion. Why did you want to be a teacher when you first began? Although sometimes we feel like all hope is lost, understand that the tides do shift. In addition, only you can make you feel a certain way. Choose to be optimistic!

Disagree in private. As mom would say, "It's best not to air your dirty laundry in public." Whether in the workplace or home, disagreements are better served when the topic is the issue and not our egos. Public dynamics bring an entirely different feel to a disagreement. Just as it would be a problem if a student stood up in your class and said, "This stinks," it is likely that public disparities feel like that for administrators. Can you disagree? Yes, but it is better to do it in a private setting.

Use the union if need be. Although there are admittedly folks whose company we enjoy, it does not give an administrator the right to bestow favors upon them. If the situation is out of hand, ask a union representative for some guidance, support, or action. Hopefully, just pointing out the inconsistency in a gentle manner will be all that it takes to restore the balance.

PRACTICAL ADVICE FOR ADMINISTRATORS

Know me; know you. The breakdown that exists between those we connect with and those we do not resides in a lack of a common bond. Great administrators get to know their members of the staff and assist them in finding their passion and purpose aside from the assessments. They hold community lunches and social events and create an atmosphere of open dialogue. Even though presented as relative extremes, we are certain that there is a connection that exists between everyone if we work diligently to find it. Great ones *try* to find favor in all.

Spread the wealth. You have the rank; spread the power among the leaders. Which leaders? Leaders you help to inspire by assisting them in finding interesting ways to satisfy both the school and their needs. For example, if Joe is a bit despondent lately, but you know he is an avid skier, maybe a little hint at running a ski club could be just the thing to rekindle his interest. By knowing the staff, you will have a better opportunity to create a buzz for folks.

Keep a chart. This may sound crazy, but a brilliant principal was having a hard time connecting with every member of his staff. What he realized is that it was so easy for him to chat with folks that had common interests (sports, fishing, etc.); he unintentionally just gravitated toward those people. His solution was to create a chart about his staff. He recorded likes, dislikes, birthdays, family events. He did his best to acknowledge what he could. He also made sure he talked (really talked) to each member of his staff every two weeks (charted the results). With this system, he held himself accountable to his goal. Way to go!

EIGHT

This Too Shall Pass

Dr. Gloria Gardner was very excited. Today, she was going to hold her first district-wide health and physical education (HPE) meeting for the Acres School District, an enormous regional entity just outside the city. Her enthusiasm could have been expected. Hired only two months prior, this would be her first opportunity to meet with the entire HPE team in one setting.

Although hosting over 110 educators for a professional development day can be nerve-wracking, Gloria was prepared. In fact, she was overprepared! She had her presentation, her handouts, and a boatload of research ready for the roll-out of the new state standards. Every minute was secure, and her attention to detail was impeccable.

To the teachers at Acres, Gloria's presentation would be a far cry from the former HPE director, Mr. Tony Brown. Tony was an "old-school" type of administrator. Having been the HPE director for the past four years, he was a caring, compassionate administrator who did more listening than talking. Although he was not much for the professional development side, folks really liked Tony, as noted by his receiving Acres' prestigious Heart Award at his retirement ceremony.

Gloria had only met Tony a few times and respected his advice on "going slow"; however, she was hired for a purpose — to implement the new state standards with the team. In realizing the superintendent had given the directive, Gloria knew what needed to be done. Besides, she believed in the standards, and her opinion of Acres' K–12 curriculum left much to be desired.

Finally, the staff started to file into the auditorium. Mr. Roland Jones was in attendance. Roland was an amazing HPE teacher. Staff and students alike had been singing his praises for the last four decades. Having taught students and now their children, he had garnered the respect and reputation of being a mainstay in the system.

Roland was also viewed by his colleagues as their voice of reason. Being a very calm and patient man, his humble demeanor and easy-going appeal brought tranquility to what had historically been a high-stress department.

As the clock struck 8:00 a.m., Gloria began her performance. She had all the bells ringing and whistles blowing, and she really felt like she was "on her game" with this material. She was! However, the teachers at Acres were not. Like deer in the headlights, folks sat bewildered staring at the screen. People at Roland's table started to get distressed.

"Nobody said anything about new standards!" one of the new teachers blurted.

"I worked all summer on my curriculum and now I have to change?" another person exclaimed as he threw his hands in the air. Predictably, the side conversations increased to a point where no one at the table could hear Gloria. Roland, however, remained quiet.

Gloria finished the first part of the presentation, and everyone was permitted an eleven-minute break. (Gloria had learned in administrator classes that if you select a specific time for break, folks would be more likely to return on time.) As other tables scattered and chattered, Roland sat. One of his colleagues pressed, "Roland, what do you make of all this?"

Like the old EF Hutton commercial, when Roland talked, everyone listened. Roland shifted in his seat and smiled. In his calming tenor, Roland said softly, "This too shall pass, my friends." And at that, a huge gasp of relief filled the table guests.

"You're right, Roland," the summer worker retorted. Roland winked.

As the day went on, Gloria gained confidence, and there were several folks excited about the changes. Yet table sixteen remained relaxed. The game plan had been established by the leader.

Gloria's enthusiasm was genuine, but obviously she had made several mistakes as a newbie. First, she needed to do a better job building more of a team approach to the new initiatives. Certainly challenging in a huge district, she could have taken the previous two months to gather ideas and plan accordingly. Even though the new standards "had to go in," the manner in which they would be received could have been negotiated. Likewise, her inability to build at least some type of relationship with a few of the key players during the summer hurt her credibility and enabled much of the side discussions to commence.

Despite Gloria's mistakes, what escapes the eye is the system's attempt to stay in balance. School systems ebb and flow, and the pace and power associated with this dynamism have many facets.

Not uncommon in the political arena, opinions shift depending on the issue, impact, and length of time people have had to deal with it. For example, think about school funding. Perhaps you live in a place where the government officials truly believe in funding the public system. Maybe they have spent the last four years desperately trying to build capacity for dynamic schools. Unfortunately, their good nature may be witnessed by some as an attempt to break the taxpayers' backs. In this case, perhaps members of the opposite party have "had enough" with this financial formula and decide to launch an all-out assault on the political machine. Tea, anyone?

This type of thinking happens in school systems, although we rarely look beyond the human beings for its origination. In other words, what if Gloria's personality (and Tony's before her) were actually establishing the "flow" of the district? For instance, suppose the current superintendent was dissatisfied with the HPE department. Although they were nice people, what if he thought that they lacked a clear vision and curriculum drive? Although he respected Tony, what if he made the decision that he was going to replace him with a real "crack fire" when he had the chance? Hello Gloria!

Now, suppose this superintendent was in his third year. What he did not know is that the former superintendent replaced Dr. Young, a spitfire HPE director who had worn out his welcome with the department and his colleagues, with Tony. In fact, what if the previous superintendent had to convince Tony to take the job to reestablish good relationships with the team? Tony agreed, and now he is being replaced. "Have a great retirement."

Neither Gloria nor her current superintendent had the hindsight to see this history. But guess who did? Roland. He had been at Acres for four decades. Four! That's a ton of movement to witness and a multitude of history to hold. As teachers with tenure, we have the benefit of witnessing the trials and tribulations of many an administrator, including their impacts on the system. But why?

Leadership comes with aspiration. When and if the time arises for departure, it can be mourned or celebrated, but should not be unexpected. Such is the life of an administrator. This is not to diminish the role of teacher-leaders. On the contrary, teacher-leaders are the backbone to the success of schools, as their impact can be felt for years.

Administrators, however, must be mobile. There are only so many jobs in one building, one district. Unlike a teacher, the administrator knows that she may be ready for a leadership position, but the system may not be ready for her. In which case, it becomes time to look anew. "This too shall pass" may be Roland's way of signifying that another ship will enter the harbor soon. (Gloria won't be here that long.)

In addition, systems rely on balance, and different people provide different pressure points to the system to secure its stability. The disconnect between teachers and administrators sometimes occurs when we fail to see that an administrator's departure may not be linked to personal agendas ("You are leaving us") but based on what is needed. Now of course people can argue that the superintendent had a personal agenda, but remember our premise (good people, good intentions).

In a profession (teaching) that values stability, it seems almost sacrilegious that someone would want to leave or that a person would have to leave to make the system better. Here is where the differences of our jobs can cause people issues when they are not personal.

Without deliberate efforts to merge tradition with current practice, districts give the impression of wholesale change instead of gradual improvement efforts. These shifts destabilize a system and throw many folks into a tizzy who were already trying their best to secure the first initiative . . . and the one before that.

PRACTICAL ADVICE FOR TEACHERS

Take initiative; stay informed. As stated prior, teacher-leaders are critical to the system, and many administrators rely on them for a host of knowledge and methodology. If your department does not meet regularly, perhaps you can suggest it should. Staying abreast of present practice helps to lessen the gap between tradition and current practices. If you cannot gain a meeting, you can always read scholarly journals, chat with a neighboring district, or talk with someone in the Intermediate Unit. Be part of the compromise between what was, what is, and what will be.

See the shift. If you were a teacher-leader with the previous administration, and now a new team is in place, you may need to see the antithesis of what was working to determine if your philosophy will jive with the new one. In other words, why was the new team put into place? This is not to say that you will automatically be replaced by "their" new leaders; however, note that folks are going to want to surround themselves with people who have common means and ends. What was "working before" for you and the school may be just the opposite for the new administrator's charge. See the *big* picture and plan accordingly.

Challenge the cliché. Although Roland's comments did bring a sense of calm to his colleagues, we cannot succumb to a defeated state to survive. "This too shall pass" unfortunately does not breed as much enlightenment as understanding why things are changing. Whether or not you agree with the change, your attitude is dictated by you. Being informed and staying positive will assist you in your journey through the best four decades of your life!

PRACTICAL ADVICE FOR ADMINISTRATORS

Know the history. When asked to build a road, the first truck on the scene cannot be the bulldozer! So many folks try to "fix" the problem without understanding its origination. Take your time. Please! Start with the survey crew. Seek out opinions and facts. Know where the issues are. Ask and you shall receive.

Plan with collective purpose. For change to be viewed as positive, it should be as anticipated as the number seven going to the number eight. We call this the *number line of change*. Every time we skip a number, we cause stress to the system. We must do our best to plan accordingly and appreciate the process. In other words, when we foster a team approach and many stakeholders have input into the planning, we create a better opportunity for a successful outcome. If you are going to dream, involve the team!

Do not falsify your expected tenure. There is no shame in wanting to be an administrator; the dishonor occurs when we fail to truthfully relay our expectations. "Better to be a highly competent boss for a few years than a mediocre one for ten!" Those who try to convince people of their longevity often create a false pretense when and if they leave, thus dooming the next administrator to a biased beginning. Give your best effort each day and allow the future to form free from fabrications.

Quick Think

Appease the issue; appreciate the individual.

II

What Administrators Say
about Teachers

NINE

It's Good for Kids

Chip wanted to help. He had always tutored students before, but now that it was not going to be compensated, he knew he had to find another part-time job to assist with his family. In being a conscientious person, he felt as if his principal was treating him differently after he said he could not tutor this year. Could this be a reality?

And so we begin this section with one of the most prolific clichés that administrators use, but often one that is seldom heard by anyone outside the administration ranks. The "it is good for kids" motto has certainly been responsible for many a void conversation and is undoubtedly a source for disconnect between management and worker. As with any cliché, there exists a hidden message behind the literal syntax. But before we explore the symbolism, let us first concentrate on the verbatim.

"It is good for kids" is a platitude that is usually utilized when a person is trying to convince another that his position is the correct one. For example, suppose an administrator was having a conversation with another administrator about whether or not to purchase student handbooks. Perhaps the person in favor of the purchase is arguing against the cost by referencing the students as collateral. In other words, the person using the cliché is setting up a situation whereby disagreeing with his point would be "not good" for kids.

Now, whether or not this is the case (maybe the books are not age appropriate and would not be a benefit to students), the user of the cliché either does not take the time to investigate or does not care to investigate. The cliché serves as a rallying cry for approval by diminishing the antithesis as hurtful. In a sense, the literal "good" is measured against the "not good," which in this scenario is every other option aside from the user's.

Of course, we all know that no one solution holds with it omnipotent virtue. Actions between human beings are seldom defined as absolutes. Culture, the way we do things, exists on various levels.[1] Technical culture exists in correctness. In simple terms, things that have technical answers are correct. For example, there is no debate that 2 + 2 = 4. It just is. Although rare in human interactions, technical answers hold with them definite ends.

Formal culture is more complex and more commonly found in human interactions. Things get done on a formal level because they are negotiated and accepted as being right.[2] For instance, wearing pink to represent cancer awareness is not a law, but an understanding in certain areas. Not doing it does not necessitate expulsion, although certain social scenes would certainly frown on the lack of acknowledgment.

For our example, the user of the cliché "it is good for kids" is trying to posture his position (buy the books) as the technical, correct answer. The cliché attempts to close the debate that would come with formal negations by stationing the kids as the leverage to the argument. However, in realizing that the opposite ("these books stink") could be true, rarely do folks just accept the cliché as simple gospel, thus promoting hard feelings or bullying tactics on the part of the initiator.

There are also hidden meanings that accompany this maxim. One such idea deals with compensation and perceived righteousness. The reality exists that some administrators believe teachers should be "doing" the extras of the job without compensation. They view the Chips of the world as folks who value the dollar more than the students. In this sense, the "it is good for kids" motto attempts to place a value on the part of the task that may be more than the individual's circumstance.

As with the initial example, Chip could really want to tutor this year and legitimately need the extra cash for his family. For a principal to hold that against him is nothing short of mean-spirited. However, what if Chip was really making an excuse? What if his family was doing fine, and he just wanted the money? Would saying no to his boss make him a ruthless gold-digger or someone who does not care about students? (Obviously, one would not condone lying to one's boss, but you get the point.)

Admit it—we all want to be paid, and there is nothing wrong with that. So why do administrators try to position teachers on the other side of virtue? Part of the reason may have to do with filling positions. It is difficult to consistently have to manage a zillion different vacancies, and in times of stress, perhaps a little guilt persuades a person into taking a position she might have not.

Yet the premise that administrators are more righteous than teachers is flawed. For example, there was an assistant superintendent who spouted off about a teacher wanting to be paid for his time, while during the same week she was negotiating a new contract that would make her the highest-paid assistant in the district's history. Please!

Face the facts. Many ideas would be "good for kids." Individual tutors would be good; smaller class sizes would be good. The list goes on and on; however, in a limited-resource environment, we must make critical decisions that regulate our ability to deliver on all possible goodness. Yet faulting someone for asking to be compensated flies in the face of the golden rule. In other words, the answer may be no, but to condemn someone for asking creates a counterculture of us versus them.

PRACTICAL ADVICE FOR TEACHERS

Balance your asks. There is a fine line between negotiating for deserved compensation and nitpicking. For example, if your lunch gets cut short by a minute because of a fire drill, do you really want to grieve this instance? Of course, events that are in direct conflict with the contract can be pursued, but you need to ask yourself if it is worth it. We need to see this relationship as give and take. Just as you may need to leave early for a doctor's appointment one day, so too may the principal need you to cover a situation in school.

A little empathy goes a long way. As stated previously, it is not easy to find folks to fulfill all of the obligations of the school. Making time to discuss the situations with your administrator might assist the two of you in developing a firm relationship and an understanding concerning each other's circumstances. Plus, you may be introduced to a new experience you never knew existed prior to the chat. Pretty cool.

Realize money does not solve it all. Although having a few extra bucks in your pocket feels good, remember why you became a teacher. In other words, this is not the profession that breeds extensive wealth. Serving the almighty dollar as a deity has destroyed many a person's spirit. Again, it is quite alright to look for opportunities to make extra compensation, but to *always* place the dollar at the head of the class may not be the best means to a favorable career. External motivations eventually overtake and diminish internal ones.

PRACTICAL ADVICE FOR ADMINISTRATORS

Stop thinking this way! There is not much more to say than what has been stated. Administrators that use the students as leverage destroy positive culture. Remember the golden rule. If it is acceptable for you to want to "better yourself," then it needs to be acceptable for teachers as well. Assume good intentions. Dismiss the consistent naggers. Do not allow their behavior to cloud your judgments when it comes to good-hearted folks looking to secure a better life for themselves and their families.

Rethink the budget. What if you could establish a system where some of the extra duties could be compensated? I know. Your boss does not want you to set a precedent; however, what is wrong with establishing mainstays with financial means? There is only so much you can ask of folks when you are standing in the free line. In other words, people who are being compensated have a different level of accountability to the project. Identify your critical initiatives and look to make them part of the financial planning of the building.

Look to build internal motivation. There is only so much money in the system. Eventually, it will diminish. You must secure other means to keep people striving for the next rung on the ladder. One of the healthiest ways to increase internal motivation is to tie it to someone's passions. Get to know your folks; find out what makes them tick. As you begin to establish this background knowledge, look for ways to include their passions in the business of the school. For instance, you may have "wanted" a chess club, but perhaps allowing Mr. Jones to run a movie club instead still gets students involved. Build capacity for dreams to become reality. This practice does not cost a dime.

NOTES

1. Edward T. Hall, *The Silent Language* (Greenwich, CT: Fawcett, 1959).
2. K. G. Clabaugh and G. E. Rozycki, *Understanding Schools: The Foundations of Education* (New York: Harper & Row, 1990).

TEN

She Beats the Kids to the Buses

Devlin High School assistant principals Toby Hunter and Josh Miller were busy filling supplemental contracts. As delegated by the principal, both Toby and Josh had the responsibility of securing over two hundred vacancies stemming from coaches and club sponsors to department heads and district liaisons. It was a daunting task, as each contract was awarded annually; however, both were up for the challenge as demonstrated by their positive nature.

The greatest resources a school has are its people. In realizing this tenet, Toby and Josh decided to discuss all 141 staff members to see if they were missing anyone who might be a great fit for one of these positions. As the morning commenced, many names made it to the whiteboard. Arguments were made, and depth charts were established.

As they reached number 79, Tau Chang's name appeared. Josh, in being the newest member of the administrative team, was unfamiliar with Tau, who apparently was a skilled writing teacher. As Josh started to place her name under the school's newspaper, Toby quickly interrupted his actions by stating, "Nope."

Josh turned and sent Toby a crinkled glance. "What's up?" he asked.

In a matter-of-fact voice, Toby stated, "She beats the kids to the buses."

At that, Josh put her name back on the table and moved to number 80. Both understood where Tau ranked in the system.

Toby Hunter remembered Tau's interview. In fact, from the entire litany of folks who applied for her position, Toby scored her the highest out of anyone on the committee. He was so thrilled to make the recommendation. Part of the reason he was excited had to do with Tau. Devlin High was in desperate need of such a skilled individual, as indicated by the dip in their state achievement scores. Tau's enthusiasm and knowledge base was just what the doctor ordered.

Another reason Toby was so excited had to do with his being the head of the committee. Sometimes principals do not allow the assistants to make personnel decisions. Knowing that Toby was a quality administrator and had been a mem-

ber of the Devlin team for years, his boss trusted his judgment to find such a dynamic candidate.

As the story goes, Tau took the job and was a marvelous instructor; however, her commitment to events outside the confines of the school day was limited at best. In the early years, Toby did his best to try to "hint" to Tau that he would love to see her help coach a team or perhaps sponsor a club. Unfortunately, those requests were left untouched. These days, Toby still believed Tau was a quality instructor, although his enthusiasm for her had admittedly diminished, especially when her car exited the parking lot each day at 2:34 p.m. In fact, Toby had once commented to another administrator that you could "set your watch" to her departure. This reality was a far cry from such initial promise.

Student involvement in schools outside the classroom can have positive impacts in student achievement (on so many levels). This same line of thinking permeates in the minds of many administrators. Principals want teachers who can extend their influence outside the classroom walls. Yet this reality is not always possible.

There are various factors that contribute to the dysfunction of this situation. Yet the prime one can be linked to the void between Tau and Toby and their lack of dialogue concerning this situation. Toby should have just asked Tau about her situation after school instead of simply assuming she was disinterested. Indeed, if he would have asked her, he might have learned that she has three children and her husband is disabled. Tau's sprint to her car is attached with her schedule. In other words, her aftercare service ends at 3:00 p.m. (Of course, Tau could have taken it upon herself to chat with Toby; however, perhaps she is not even aware of the animosity that has been formed by her expedient exits.)

We cannot fault Toby too much for his feelings of being let down by Tau. Maybe he really "sold her" as the next big thing. Maybe the principal reminds him when they are on bus duty together and witness her leaving, "That one was your hire." Who knows? Anticipation burst by reality can be disturbing.

In addition, it is quite a task to fill vacancies with quality people. And the added benefit of having these folks as employees is apparent (clearances completed, influence with students, know the grounds, policies, etc.). Seeing teachers and administrators in a different venue can and does provide students a fresh lens to judge us and, more importantly, connects with the mission of the school. Yet, in today's whirlwind of activity, we sometimes forget the core of our responsibility. Here is where the disconnect starts.

Primary function (PF) represents the most meaningful purpose an individual brings to a system by considering both the impact that function has on the system and the void associated with its absence. This type of thinking centers us in establishing the root means and desired ends to the system for which we are servicing.

PF in simple terms is our job responsibility at its most basic point. For instance, although it would have been wonderful for Tau to be able to coach three sports a year, her most meaningful obligation is to teach children how to write well. This is not to say that she could not be an outstanding basketball coach, but the system needs her to first be an outstanding writing instructor.

Please do not draw any cryptic conspiracies from the previous paragraph. I am not saying that teacher-coaches should not coach because they should only concentrate on their subject and we should leave the coaching to those who will only focus on that. As stated previously, there are a plethora of other factors that supply wins for kids besides the outcome to the games.

The issue with PF stems from the fact that a teacher's jobs are as infinite as the solar system. Because we influence so many facets of the success of a child, not only is it difficult to quantify our impacts (tell that to the politicians who want to rate us on just scores), but it also becomes an expected outcome that we will continue to give even at the detriment of ourselves, our families, and so on.

It is fine for Toby to be a little disappointed that Tau cannot coach, but he (or any other administrator) should not label a teacher as shiftless if they must attend to duties outside of the school. Labeling laziness without cause creates ill will between folks. Likewise, it slanders people's names without solid evidence for its inception.

PRACTICAL ADVICE FOR TEACHERS

Explain your circumstances. Being proactive is a valued skill, and one that will serve you well in and out of school. Having a tiny tête-à-tête with your administrator concerning your situation can and does breed understanding and empathy. Who knows, maybe the two of you have more in common than you think. Or perhaps there is a way for you to be involved in a different manner. Worlds of possibilities exist when we take the time to talk to one another.

Don't cut the buses off. Sometimes the manner in which we do what we do creates an aura that permeates to our person. In other words, actions are more readily judged as negative when they are performed by negative people. This may seem like a simple concept, but it is one that is oftentimes neglected in busy environments. *We model all of our lives.* In realizing this idea, be cognizant with the manner of your actions. It is one thing to *roll* early and quite another to *rock* on out of there!

There are other ways to assist. As mentioned previously, there are various needs for students. Just because you cannot dedicate time after school does not mean that you cannot help out in other arenas. Make the time to get to know what is going on in the building. For instance, holding special lunch sessions, assembly programs, or theme days are all ways to make your presence known.

PRACTICAL ADVICE FOR ADMINISTRATORS

Focus on primary functions. Human commodities can become limiting when they are rare and in demand. Rank and prioritize who can do what and why. Focus on fulfilling the essential needs with the most qualified of individuals and allow them space to create. Taxing the folks that we always tag decreases opportunities for others. However, if a person cannot go the extra mile outside the classroom, but is an Olympic sprinter within, cherish the gold they bring to the students each and every day.

Have one-on-one check-in sessions. One fantastic idea that was shared with me was one-on-one check-ins. This concept, although not earth shattering, is a fantastic way to get to know the staff outside the realm of PF. In focusing these meetings on more general topics (How is the family? Summer plans?), a more personal approach to the work can commence. Plus, these types of settings also provide time for "what if" moments that can be an excellent source of gathering feedback concerning special topics. Just be sure not to present as if the only reason is for a personal one and that the family chatting is nothing more than small talk.

What if a person was intentionally uninvolved? This situation can be tricky in that we cannot force someone to do what she does not wish to do. (Yes, I know. Bosses can force people to do lots of things. Remember the premise.) Building the right conditions for involvement may be a plan of action. The more you can create a situation where people can follow their passions, the more likely they are to put the time into that endeavor. Initiatives are best served when they are good for both the organization and the individuals.

Quick Think

Failure fuels the fluid mind.

ELEVEN

Getting the Buy-In

Drinking the Kool-Aid

Jody Welch was a dedicated, hardworking administrator who supervised the K–12 science department in the Geary School District. Although Geary was a rural school district, this was not to say that they did not have their issues. For several months, folks in the science department had been debating which science kits were going to be selected to complement next year's curriculum revision tied to the new standards. Unfortunately for the teachers at Geary, these conversations were devoid of one key ingredient. That key was Jody.

Jody was not participating in these conversations at all. In fact, she did not even think they were occurring. Since she had announced the district's intent to change programming to the staff, she had been diligently researching potential resources for science labs (kits). In her mind, everyone had a job to do. The teachers teach; supervisors supervise. In being the leader of the team, she took it as her responsibility to complete the research. Pretty nice of her.

As May approached, she had completed her work and had unofficially selected a company. The reason her decision was unofficial was because one week prior, she had announced to the team that a committee would be forming to discuss the current situation and decide on the appropriate action.

This was a very exciting time for her and her department, or so she thought. As she gave her report at the biweekly administrative leadership team meeting, she mentioned the plan to the other folks. Everyone seemed good with the decision and felt that she had really "sunk her teeth" into the research. When asked how she was going to get the team to select the chosen company, she simply stated that she would have to "get the buy-in" from the team.

No one batted an eye.

The "buy-in" has to be one of the most celebrated phrases in administrator verbiage. Married to its more recent cousin (drinking the Kool-Aid), these slogans capture the heart of the administrator-teacher divide, as they position people to be pods instead of human beings.

Managers make critical decisions all the time, and a supervisor having influence over which science kit to use does not seem to be that out of the ordinary. Some would even say that this type of work is part of a supervisor's job. (Jody certainly felt that way.) Yet the separation in this situation started prior to any science selection; it began with a philosophy that does not support the Theory of Relevance (TOR).

TOR is a term used to define instances where decisions should be influenced by those who have to carry out the decision. As mentioned earlier, technical culture has to do with correctness.[1] People perform actions on a technical level because they work. For example, opening a door works much better when one uses the handle instead of just trying to walk through it like Herman Munster. (I just love it when Fred Gwynne slams through that door.) Technical culture works.

Formal culture, conversely, is negotiated between individuals. This culture impacts human interactions. In other words, rare are the times when technical answers exist when dealing with human beings. Formal culture depends on context. What is right for some folks may not be right for others. Hence, parleys are part of a formal plan.

Obviously, Jody was not in favor of the notion of parley. Nor did she comprehend the TOR. People who are closest to the actual "doing" of the work should have the most tangible say in noncrisis situations because they are going to be the ones who have to "do/use" the decision. In this situation, the TOR suggests that Jody should not be the one selecting science kits because, ultimately, the teachers will have to utilize them.

In this situation, Jody made a technical decision instead of holding a formal process. She shortcut the method by establishing a "correct" answer in place of one that could have been right. How do we know this to be the case? Options. In other words, since there were options to this resolution, there was more than one way to attain the results.

What might have been the better plan is to allow the teachers to see which kit really "worked" for them. In other words, perhaps by allowing the process to commence, the teachers would have selected a resource that was usable instead of one that met some type of fabricated researched targets. Instead, Jody started and ended with research and dismissed the practicality of the decision.

Sometimes educational experts hinder process because they anticipate an argument. These are often the people who either bring an enormous amount of research to the table or simply plan a course of action that suppresses an open process. Here is where the contrived committee is born.

When reviewing this chapter, folks have solicited a possible solution to this problem. We can learn so much from our brethren outside of the educational world. For example, have you bought a hat lately? Seriously, have you purchased a hat in the last few months? If so, how did you buy it? Did you research the best possible caps? How they are made? Price comparison, and so on? Or did you put it on to see how it fit and looked?

Don't get me wrong. Research is great and needed in all environments; however, at some point, even the research will yield a few choices. After that, how do we make decisions? You guessed it, the formal process (What is right for us? How do I look?) combines with the technical one (this hat fits; it works). Here is where we live.

Have you ever had a teacher say, "Just tell me what you want me to do"? This statement summarizes the frustration that accompanies confusion and mistrust. Teachers that have been "burned by the process of artificial collaboration" tend to move to the lowest common denominator of human interaction—submission. Yet administrators fault teachers for this response by turning a blind eye toward the frustration and believing that the person is just being negative.

As administrators, we need to trust our staff. We need to exist in process. When we believe we can just "sway" others to thinking the way we do, we ignore free will and set a course for destinations that do not exist.

P.S. Remember those science kits? Take a guess where you can find them these days. Rank and power are beautiful ideals, are they not?

PRACTICAL ADVICE FOR TEACHERS

Believe it's real. Losing hope when it comes to being able to give your opinion is a lonely place, and one that can destroy our drive. We must fight against the tendency to believe that all committee decisions are already decided. Just because the last seven committees appear to be contrived does not necessarily mean that number eight will be. Hope springs eternal.

Ask the tough questions. It is understood that folks usually do not want to create a negative reputation when it comes to their bosses; however, it is perfectly fine practice to solicit answers to questions that need to be answered. Now, the manner in which we seek such justifications can and does have a ton to do with their outcomes. Remember, no one wants to be embarrassed, especially in public. Nonetheless, neglecting to ask the questions will only cause more harm when one sulks about them in the future. Just remember, ask the question to secure the information, not to try to wound someone or demonstrate that we "know more" than the next person. Those bully tactics are so played.

Participate in the process. If you are going to complain that your administrator team does not want your opinion, you cannot hang in the shadows (and complain) when a process does come to be. (I guess you can do this, but that would be a real shame.) Sign up and be heard. Stay positive and support the process. You may not have your way completely, but that is the beauty of détente.

PRACTICAL ADVICE FOR ADMINISTRATORS

Understand culture. Leaders who fail to understand human interactions fail. Plain and simple! Put people first. Every time we lead with items instead of people, we create distance between ourselves and the team. Build capacity for building. That is what great leaders do.

In crisis, decide. In peace, negotiate. You have the rank and possess the right to make decisions and have those decisions accomplished. Yet it is best to apply this logic when in crisis. In times of peace, look to secure a good to great approach, whereby you allow for inquiry and investigation to guide continuous improvement.

Spread the word about TOR. The Theory of Relevance must be learned. To neglect context and technical expertise creates waste (science kits hint). The team exists for many reasons. They are responsible for the implementation of said decisions. To ignore their input dooms culture, climate, and careers for both teachers and administrators.

NOTE

1. K. G. Clabaugh and G. E. Rozycki, *Understanding Schools: The Foundations of Education* (New York: Harper & Row, 1990).

TWELVE

You Work for a District, Not a School

You could set your watch by Dr. Valerio's arrival at the buildings. Dr. Valerio was the human resources director in Colonial School District, and it was his job to inform the teachers of transfers following the April staffing meetings.

During the staffing summits, the needs of the district were discussed as they related to student enrollment, section numbers, and so on. Principals and central office folks met for days to solve the yearly fluctuation that occurred in enrollment. Meetings were intense, as the process of securing one's team was personal at times. Inevitably, whether by consensus or concession, decisions were made and game plans were set for the following school year. Here is where Dr. Valerio made his bones.

Once the final staffing sheets were finalized, it was Dr. Valerio's job to inform staff of transfers. (In this district, building-to-building transfers were completed by the central office; in-building transfers, typically grade-level or subject-level, were completed by the principals.) These discussions would always occur during the second week in May.

From veteran to rookie, everyone knew about Dr. V's visits. In fact, you could almost hear the emails ping and the phones ring when his silver XC60 Volvo arrived. Jonathon Holst, a tenth grade language teacher at Colonial High School, was familiar with the ritual. Being a French instructor, he had several visits from Dr. V. during his tenure, as the language numbers and interest can sometimes vary.

When Dr. Valerio arrived at CHS, Jon did his best to try and calm folks down, especially Grace Rice, a new math instructor. Grace was certain that she was going to be moved. Being the newest member of the department, she noticed the dip in enrollment. Heck, she was a statistics teacher, and trend lines were her lifelines.

Predictably, the office summoned for Grace, and at that, she burst into tears. Jon did his best to comfort her during the seemingly endless trip to the office.

"I don't understand," Grace explained. "What did I do wrong?"

Jonathon worked diligently to defend her honor. He cited numerous instances where Grace had gone above and beyond, but this comfort went to no avail. She was too far gone for any pity accolades.

Once Grace was in Dr. Valerio's presence, he proceeded to tell her she was being transferred to Stark Middle School, one of the four middle schools that fed into CHS. When he asked if she had any questions, Grace asked, "How could this happen?"

In a calm and steady voice, Dr. Valerio said, "Because you work for a district, Mrs. Rice. Not a school."

Although there are some districts that have clauses in their contracts that prohibit transfers, there are many others that do not. For them, being sent to another school is a possibility, especially where enrollments sway and class selection is contingent on supply and demand. Such was the case at Colonial.

Assumedly, the good news for this scenario is that the district is responsible to find a job for people, even if one does not exist in their current location. However, when discussing this issue with colleagues from the business world, rest assured that empathy does not run abundant. The "here today, gone tomorrow" mantra is an occupational reality, and many folks have been forced to find employment elsewhere. Yet, despite this type of hardship for our working brethren, facing change is not an easy proposition, and Grace's reaction is certainly not uncommon.

When entering into the issue of transfers, administrators usually use one of two tactics. The first one deals with change itself. For example, how many times have you been in a situation where someone is telling you that "change is good"? There must be hundreds of variations that you have weathered during the course of your tenure, and many times these changes do turn out to be positive. However, just because the last variation was affirmative does not necessarily mean the next one will be.

Change might be good, but time and impact play a part in the acceptance or rejection of one's circumstance. And this is certainly the case for educators. Consider that teachers are affirmed for being in control. This is not to say that they are control freaks, but the organization and critical planning it takes to assist people in the learning process is immense. Days and years are spent perfecting routines that yield incredible benefits for their students. And all of that work can be wiped away in an instance in the name of "change is good."

The second way that administrators define a transfer is by taking a business approach to the situation. "You work for a district, not a school" is another way of saying, "It's just business." Less positive than "change is good," this cliché lets the teacher know that she should be lucky to still have a job, a fabulous way to prepare someone for a fresh start! (Not quite.)

As we have discussed, teachers are fortunate to have situations where they can be afforded other positions in the system; nevertheless, both of these justifications diminish the human connections that accompany human interactions. For instance, when you travel overnight, what do you usually bring with you? Toothbrush, toothpaste, clean clothes, cell phone, shoes, credit cards, and so on. Although we try to pack light, inevitably, you will usually tally ten to twelve essential items for your jaunt. And that's just for one night!

Now imagine what has been acquired during the course of one's tenure in a building for just five years. Think those items are fitting in a travel case? The amount of materials we accumulate is extraordinary, and yet, in many places, we are judged for keeping "too much stuff." Administrators need to realize they cannot have it both ways. If you want teachers to be innovative, then we have to allow for luggage that comes with learned lessons.

In addition to the items, think about the memories and connections that were made. Marriages, babies, grandchildren, and so on! To dismiss these moments in a swipe of "you work for a district" demonstrates a total lack of compassion. Lives are being lived in our schools. As the students, families, and administrators come and go, the constant is, and always will be, the teachers. As one leaves the flock, it is only natural to feel a sense of loss for a system that sustains because of teachers' constancy.

PRACTICAL ADVICE FOR TEACHERS

In every change lies opportunity. Being transferred can be a traumatic experience, and one that causes great stress for us. However, once you have had time to process and mourn the move, try to view this as an opportunity to become reborn. Whether first looked on as a negative, a change can provide us with a chance to lead new initiatives or learn new practices. Not that we need to be preached to that change is good; it certainly can be given time and a fluid mind.

Take the support. Some folks become so angry when they are transferred that they almost become hermits. Do yourself and your colleagues a favor and take the support that comes with moving to a new environment. Just as you want to have a positive experience, the people at the building where you are going certainly do not want some crabapple to ruin their spirit. Meet people. Sit down with the principal and chat. Smile. It will go a long way!

Appreciate each day. As Robert Frost put so eloquently, "Nothing gold can stay." Take each day as a precious gift that can be dimmed. Appreciate what you have while you have it. Build your legacy from day one.

PRACTICAL ADVICE FOR ADMINISTRATORS

People first. How would you want to be treated if the time came for your transfer? Don't outthink yourself. Stop hiding behind protocol or fear of lawsuits and be a human being. Treat people with dignity and respect. They won't follow you because of what you know. They will open their minds and hearts up to the possibility of leading with you only if you show them you care.

Give people time to process. In wanting to fix things quickly, we sometimes create more hurt than good. Remember, too much good can be a bad thing. Give people time to process. Just as teachers need to value wait time, so too do administrators need to plan for process time. Adults have so many details to decide. Trying to remedy every ailment at the speed of light produces shorts in the system.

Offer assistance and support. Again, build your leadership on compassion and empathy. Help pack boxes; move a desk or cabinet. Sure, you do not have to do it, but it costs nothing to be nice. Plus, guess who is watching?

Quick Think

Passions crave actions; otherwise, they are just words.

THIRTEEN

She Has No Walls

There were not many professional educators like Gwen Murphy. Gwen was a kindergarten teacher at Brighten Elementary School, and had been gracing the hallways of Brighten for the past thirty-two years. Nowadays, it is rare to find someone who has spent her entire career in one school let alone twenty-nine years in the same classroom. Her success was quite an accomplishment, especially being the oldest of seven children in her family, but the only one to earn a college degree. Obviously, her career was a source of great pride for them.

Gwen was a soft soul in the classroom. She adored her students, and they reciprocated by working hard to learn their lessons. Gwen utilized a calm and caring voice, and the students always cooperated with her instructions. It was a match made in paradise. Unfortunately, not everyone at Brighten believed that Gwen was sent from the heavens.

Gwen had a tendency to utilize her "kindergarten voice" with everyone. Although no one believed that Gwen was purposefully being bold or bossy, her communications did not resemble such sweet discussion but more of sour soliloquies. In fact, the new principal, Greta Trude, would dread their exchanges.

Whenever Greta would notice Gwen heading toward her, she would do her best David Blake and vanish through the side door or adjacent lobby. Even the administrative assistants would scoff whenever Gwen did catch up with her because they knew how Greta felt.

Greta saw Gwen as an asset to the school, but she always wondered why Gwen felt it necessary to treat everyone like children. Actually, one time she even described Gwen to another group of principals as someone who likes to "play god." Of course, this reference was not to be taken in a literal sense, but the other folks knew what Greta was saying — Gwen's classroom had no walls.

The old "she is treating us like one of her students" adage is alive and well in today's schools. Like the earlier version, "She has no walls" cap-

73

tures the essence of control gone awry by positioning the person as a dictator (even with a pleasant voice). However, before we can begin to suggest how to adjust to this circumstance, we must first discover its origination.

By all accounts, Gwen Murphy is not a malicious woman. Nor is she the type of person that is believed to be hoarding power for self-gain. Gwen is a kindergarten teacher, and in being a kindergarten teacher, she is used to directing. All totaled, Gwen has been directing for 5,760 days. That's 43,200 hours—a heck of a long time to be the center of attention to five-year-olds!

If we consider the core of a five-year-old, these are some of the most positive, eager-to-learn bunnies in the whole bunch. Channeling that energy is certainly a full-time task, and one where Gwen thrived; nonetheless, to work in that type of environment, one must realize that five-years-olds are also some of the most needy, non-self-sufficient students in the system (next to seniors in quarter number four). Spend an hour in a kindergarten classroom, and you will begin to realize what type of effort it takes to survive in this environment. Now consider spending 43,200 hours!

Gwen did what came naturally to her. She was used to giving positive direction, speaking in a friendly, firm voice, and setting the suggested course of action for almost every situation. The term *guided discovery* certainly emphasized the word *guided*! Yet what created such success for Gwen in the classroom is the very same structure that caused so much stress outside of it.

DID YOU EVER REALIZE THAT YOUR GREATEST STRENGTH CAN ALSO BE YOUR GREATEST WEAKNESS?

So much of what we view as an asset in one arena may be a detriment in another. Such is the case for context. For example, a friendly fellow who has a knack for making people laugh may have just used this type of tactic to entice his now-wife to date him. Yet do not be surprised if his sense of humor is the source of controversy every time he tells a joke to another woman. Here, the motivation (hidden meaning) behind the joke is what is being judged. The wife may think, "Scott told me jokes to make me laugh to get me to like him. If he is telling jokes to someone else, I wonder. . . ."

In the later situation, Scott's desire to make people laugh (a perceived asset) may be the actual sticking point of an otherwise-successful marriage. Unless Scott's spouse explains how this situation makes her feel, Scott may go right on being funny without realizing he is hurting his marriage with each jest.

This may also be a similar situation for Gwen. Gwen may believe she is doing exactly what makes her successful. She may think, *It works in the classroom; it should work here.* Unfortunately, if she cannot witness the divide, and no one is willing to point it out to her, we acquire a situation that has no end.

Social conditioning is alive and well in schools today. The patterns that exist in our lives are replicated when they afford us success. Although not with ill intent, Gwen's reality is to be the mother hen to her flock. This tendency to continue to "mother" people is not necessarily a god complex, but a situation that was born over time and proven to work.

The key to this situation resides in our constant need to keep ourselves in check. What works in one venue may not yield the same results in the next.

PRACTICAL ADVICE FOR TEACHERS

See the pattern. As you continue in your journey to build a legacy of positive resolve, be sure to take notice of the patterns that exist in your life. Can you see occurrences where one form of success may not fit another? Folks that are attuned to such intricacies often look to promote some type of change in their lives.

Leave the teacher's hat in the classroom. This is such a difficult crutch to overcome because we are so passionate about teaching that it feels almost sacrilegious not to teach no matter the location or audience. We must realize it is fantastic to have passion for our profession, but the best methodology we can use (both in and out of the classroom) is to allow the learner to pilot the learning. *The more we can assist instead of insist, the better relationships will be.*

Solicit feedback. Maybe not at first, but perhaps Gwen did notice that Greta was treating her a bit differently than the rest of her colleagues. Not that she did anything wrong or intentional, but we must be willing to acknowledge that other people may have different opinions. Here, we are not suggesting that Gwen needed to change, but that soliciting the information surrounding the issue may have offered a different perspective.

PRACTICAL ADVICE FOR ADMINISTRATORS

Ducking through doors is for cowards. How old are we? If an administrator has an issue with a teacher, she needs to have a dialogue with that teacher. The triangulation (talking about it with other people) has to stop. How can we expect Gwen or anyone to adjust if we are unwilling to be honest? Of course, we can and should discuss these issues with a sincerity that accompanies a teammate; however, to just ignore the issue and pretend it is not there is bogus. Come on, Greta.

Teach this pattern. Again, one of the greatest opportunities we have in this profession is to be lifelong learners. Social conditioning that occurs can be veiled, but also a powerful force in our lives. Book studies, professional-development chats, and scholarly articles are all ways that you can bring this topic to light without offending anyone. Instead of just thinking someone has a god complex (especially since actually making that judgment of someone is more in line with what a deity would do), be proactive and plan for robust discussions.

Lead with compassion. We all have our faults. All of us! To judge someone without an opportunity for them to respond positions you as an insensitive leader. For just as the administrative assistants were laughing with you about Gwen, realize that they might be wondering what you are making fun of them about and to whom. We reap what we sow. Although there are times when difficult decisions must be made and communicated, it costs nothing to lead with the heart.

Quick Think

It might be business, but it is also the business of someone's life.

FOURTEEN

The Buck Stops Here!

No Surprises

Distinctions in rank and power often litter the educational system like the millions of mussels assorted on the beaches of Cape Cod. (Step on one of those shells, and you will know who is in charge.) Realizing that "here" is within each of us is the key to collaborative leadership and a tip of the cap to the Theory of Relevance. Moreover, the administrator's ability to limit the amount of muscle used with attaining actions will make for a better outcome for all. But this advice is easier heard than followed.

Cheryl Grimes was a school nurse at Littleton Elementary School in the Webber School District. This was her fifteenth year at Littleton, and she was one of the founding members for the outdoor education excursion that the sixth grade students took each year. One of the reasons that Cheryl was so involved with the trip was linked to her passion for adventure. She was an avid hiker, biker, and traveler. Likewise, her passion for students to be "on the move" was relentless.

Dr. David Rooney was not much for adventure. Being in his third year at Littleton, he was not much for physical movement either. David was about the numbers. He believed he was hired to "fix" Littleton's scores on the state assessment, and he saw this three-day trip as a slash into instructional time. Although he realized the tradition of the school was too powerful to just eliminate the outing, he secretly wished it would go away.

During this year's trip, Brady Barnes, a sixth grade student, accidently fell. Cheryl did her best to check him out. She examined him, asked him a ton of questions, and was assured that he was fine. (In fact, he was performing pushups to prove he was okay.) Cheryl decided to allow him to return to his cabin.

As fate would have it, Brady's arm continued to hurt him after the trip had concluded. A week later, his parents took him to the doctor, where they found out that Brady had a slight fracture. He would be fine, but would have to have a cast for a few weeks. Brady's mother informed the school the next day. Here is where the story bursts.

When Dr. Rooney's secretary informed him of the goings on, he exploded. "Get me Ms. Grimes!" he shouted. His secretary tried to explain to him that Brady was going to be okay, but the good doctor was hearing none of that.

He retorted with a stern, "The buck stops here Mrs. Jones. Right here!" He pointed at himself so that the effect spoke in unison with his words. Dr. Rooney enjoyed being demonstrative.

As Cheryl entered the office, she could tell something was awry. Dr. Rooney started with his typical "How many times do I have to tell you people that I do not like surprises?"

Cheryl did her best to listen and stay calm during his recapping the story. When asked, she explained exactly what happened and what she did in response to the events; however, Dr. Rooney was simply not interested in her side. As she spoke, he could not help but to think if this trip was not a reality, there would be no issues with it.

Brady's parents were not looking for retribution, but Dr. Rooney was. He took this opportunity to wage an all-out assault on the trip. He did not succeed in eliminating it (as the teachers, curriculum supervisors, families, and even the superintendent believed it was of value), but his point was made. From now on, even if someone received a hang nail, he wanted to know and be involved in the future planning. His trust for his staff had departed.

Do you know anyone like Dr. Rooney? Sadly, there are those in educational systems that resemble this type of tyrant leader. In chapter 2, we reviewed the tenets of the administrator who needs to control everything and everyone, but Dr. Rooney's behavior speaks of a different type of problem that exists in our schools today. Besides his lack of people skills, Dr. Rooney embodies one of the greatest destroyers of morale in a school—principals who are a team of one.

It is not that uncommon for a boss to want a "heads-up" when someone thinks an event could have the potential to be troublesome. Indeed, this is a practice that exists in many places of hierarchy and should not be viewed as a negative unto itself. If teachers are looking to be reinforced from their administrators, such support would be more solid if the principal knew the background of the issue prior to it becoming one. No one likes to be blindsided, especially when a child is injured.

Yet Dr. Rooney's philosophy that "he is the only one who can judge" thwarts even this practice. By establishing himself as the absolute authority, the message sent to the rest of the staff is that they are incapable of making value decisions. When the administrator truly believes that leadership is isolated from the people that have direct contact with the students, both surprises and known instances become a source of judgment and retribution.

WHY DO SO MANY ADMINISTRATORS FEEL THAT THEY HAVE TO USE FORCE TO MOVE HUMAN BEINGS?

Could there be a feeling of insecurity that exists the minute we step outside of the pack, the day we exit the perceived safety of the union? Maybe. But this anxiety is not mandated. In other words, perhaps we are choosing to exist in fear and back ourselves into a corner, much like a tiger does when threatened. Perhaps we await the anticipated battle, ready to pounce at the first sign of danger.

I once knew a lady who spent oodles of cash on furnishing her house with the most expensive, lavish décor only to not allow anyone to sit on it when they visited. Turns out, her close friends stopped attending her social functions, as they grew tired of standing and wondering why they were not good enough to deserve a seat.

Many a blank page resides within a would-be artist's notebook.

The buck does not stop. It exists within a collaborative vision, a team approach. Those who see the magic of a shared mission thrive; those who do not, never even open the bottles of paint.

PRACTICAL ADVICE FOR TEACHERS

Keep the principal informed. There will be times in your career where something has the potential of going wrong. On those occasions, it is perfectly fine to inform the principal that a situation has potential. Keeping people in the loop is a practice that assists many in their quest to stay under the radar. The key is balance. The boss does not need to know every little thing (unless he is like Dr. Rooney). Sending a simple email may be just the thing. Yet the best bet is to ask the principal how she may want to be informed and for what subjects.

What to do with the Dr. Rooneys of the world. This is certainly not an easy proposition. If you believe that you are being bullied by an administrator, then you have the right to speak with human resources and involve the union. However, if your principal is not a bully but a blowhard, following the known protocol may just be the best tactic. In other words, if Dr. Rooney wants to know every little detail, then give it to him in a professional and polite manner. There might come a time when you could have an honest chat with him. If this situation presents itself, follow the golden rule and go for it. Remember, even the Rooneys are insecure.

When in doubt, get assistance. Cheryl used her professional training and judgment to handle the situation. If there was any doubt on her part, it would have been best to call 911. In working with children, safety is job one. When we feel that a situation has potential to cause harm (or more harm going forward), it is best to solicit advice from someone who holds more knowledge. Likewise, staying abreast of different legal decisions is also a solid practice for folks working in the public.

PRACTICAL ADVICE FOR ADMINISTRATORS

Survey the team. Administrators need feedback to grow as leaders. Certainly, your boss can provide you with critical areas for improvement, but the real people that know your pluses and minuses are the staff. Using an anonymous survey with them demonstrates trust. (Of course, it would be wonderful to have names on a survey, but until your building gets to that place, better to use an instrument now instead of waiting.) Gather the results and form a team to go after the positive changes.

Define the surprises. Leaving the staff guessing as to what they should and should not tell you causes anxiety and mistrust. Do your best to define instances of information that you would want to know. Maybe it is as simple as any safety-related issue. Ask some of your staff what they think. Maybe there are situations with parents that they also feel you might need to know. Work together to define the guidelines to ensuring surprises are kept to a minimum.

Surprise . . . there will be surprises. Even with a guideline, human judgments are not foreseeable. If something does occur that you wish you knew sooner, do your best to handle the situation first without judging the person involved. At a later time, talk to that person. Try to see her rationale. Maybe there was a good reason for not informing you. Maybe not. Yet this type of calm, trust-building approach will go a long way in setting the stage for your relation with her and the rest of the staff.

Life is unpredictable; dealing with its nuisances in a composed manner breeds confidence.

Quick Think

The devil does not reside in the details; negotiations of right foster friction and flexibility.

III

Clichés We All Use

FIFTEEN

Thrown Under the Bus!

Being the principal of Jameswood High School, Fred Reilly enjoyed meeting his teachers on opening day. In being a simple man, he employed a simple message: "I reward loyalty." And he meant it.

Many a staff member at Jameswood could attest to this maxim. Fred was not one to mince words, and his expectation of trustworthiness could be felt from the classrooms to the faculty rooms. In having worked for Fred for several years, Jill Manish knew her principal. She realized that others had suffered consequences in the past when it came to "speaking up" to him. However, on this particular day, she felt compelled to finally give her honest opinion.

Two days prior, Jill had been the faculty representative at the PTO meeting. During the meeting, several members of the parents group were upset with the spring concert. It seems as though the parents were a bit unnerved by some of the song choices and wanted to know how the selection process worked. Fred, in a very abrupt manner, told the group that he had "nothing to do" with song selection, and that if there was a problem, they were going to have to speak with Ms. Foster, the chorus teacher.

This situation bothered Jill. She thought to herself, How can a person who wants loyalty from the teachers be so quick to throw one of his own under the bus? The next day, Jill overheard a few teachers at another table talking about how Ms. Foster had to skip lunch to meet with a group of upset chorus families.

Feeling just awful, Jill could not help herself. "I was there," she said softly.

The teachers at the other table asked her to clarify. And she did in detail. With that, some of the more veteran teachers became incensed. "This is the last straw!" one stammered as she rose to her feet. "Trust is a two-way street." As the bell rang, the few who remained vowed that something needed to be done. Jill, now really nervous, knew her name would be mentioned if any retort was to occur. She needed to do something. But what?

Colloquial phrases infiltrate every system, but none of them seem to come with the same irritation as "thrown under the bus." Part of the reason this cliché speaks to us in schools has to do with the metaphor. Buses are part of our existence. Without these mean machines, we would be underserving a host of our clients' needs. Yet the real charge comes from the underlying issue of disloyalty and the assumption of assistance.

Ask any teacher what she wants from her principal and the answer will probably be "support!" In knowing that we deal with the public day in and day out, the likelihood of a transgression occurring that would question our judgment is inevitable. Teachers look for the support of the principal when dealing with these types of situations because the assumption is that no ill action would have occurred on purpose.

Ironically, ask a principal what she would want from her boss, and the answer would most likely be the same. In fact, as we ascend through the realms of management, who wouldn't look to garner support from the direct line of authority? Again, this type of loyalty is built on the hypothesis that the people would not intentionally offend. However, can loyalty be given blindly or must it be earned?

Clearly, the previous anecdote speaks of various mistakes that were made by the principal. Fred's first fault dealt with his original philosophy. To believe that people are loyal on word alone creates an imbalance of power and fosters the opposite of the intended act. In other words, just because the boss "demands" loyalty does not necessarily mean folks will be able to give it to him unconditionally. Rank alone does not garner absolution from inaccuracies.

Those who demand allegiance based on name alone fail to realize that human beings have the ability to think, reason, and judge. Of course it goes without saying that it is never a great idea to slam the boss in public, but to assume that everyone is going to be loyal to you just because you are the boss diminishes your ability to truly lead by placing rank above power.

We are witnessing this line of thinking in every facet of the educational system these days. No longer do students just offer blind devotion to their teachers based on rank alone. Some would say that this fact is the ruination of schools. How can we teach when those to be taught do not value the hierarchy of order?

However, maybe the shift can be considered a positive in light of what it forces us to do as teachers. In simple terms, the days of just showing up and going through the motions are long gone. Students, like teachers, have opinions, likes, and dislikes and can make judgments. In the days of texts and tweets, supplying feedback to the teacher is easier than ever. Admittedly, not all of this feedback is positive, but the point still serves. The ability to assume loyalty just because of rank is diminishing. (Again, the premise must serve here. The assumption stands that folks are good natured. No one is trying to hurt anyone or be disrespectful.)

The second blunder Fred made, and probably a more obvious one, has to do with his shifting the problem to his chorus teacher's lap. This is not to say that Ms. Foster was not the one responsible for selecting the songs. Maybe she was. Maybe there was a process that she was supposed to follow, and she failed. Maybe Fred was annoyed that she did not follow said protocol and that's why he blurted out her name. The only people who really know the truth are Fred and Ms. Foster. But to the innocent onlookers like Jill, we can imagine what that must have felt like: "The wheels on the bus go round and round." [1]

Nevertheless, it is not uncommon for folks to want us to solve problems at the point of inception. In other words, it stands to reason that if Ms. Foster did indeed select the music, it would be difficult for Fred to defend her thought process unless he was directly involved. Within this line of thinking, perhaps going to the source would be the best plan of action. Unfortunately, Fred's curt identification of Ms. Foster as the point person sat wrong with Jill. In her opinion, Fred did not "take one for the team" (another cliché that is built on loyalty and ownership).

Certainly, Fred could have provided cover for Ms. Foster fairly easily. He simply could have said, "I will find out" and done just that. His decision to quickly identify another member of the team and "deflect" the ire gave the impression of being disloyal. Combine this action with a person who demands loyalty (but does not return it) and you have a pretty despondent situation.

As one can imagine, this school has other issues besides this particular departure (a little bus humor). Loyal actions earn loyal members of a team. Once more, when we do make a mistake (e.g., Fred did partake in selecting the songs), then we must be willing to own the deed. Those who jockey for position away from potential conflict usually create a reputation of being a coward. Not a positive situation for anyone.

As fate would have it, Jill scheduled a meeting with Fred. During the meeting, she explained how she felt and that she believed this type of occurrence could hurt his reputation with the staff. Fred listened. As she concluded with her account, Fred stood up and said, "Thank you for your honesty."

"Wow!" she thought. "That was not what I expected." Only time will tell if it was heartfelt, but the fact that Fred made a b-line toward the chorus room was a really positive sign.

PRACTICE ADVICE

Never demand loyalty. As a matter of your practice, look to secure loyalty based on your actions. Remember, talk is cheap when it comes to earning someone's trust. The more you can do what you say you are going to do, the more you will create a sustainable imprint. As a hint to this type of thinking, assume that what you are about to say needs to be justified. In other words, instead of decreeing, offer opportunities for opposing views. People do not become loyal to those who always have to be correct. They become tired of them.

Own what you own. Why are we so afraid of making mistakes? When we screw it up, just say we screwed it up. Nothing creates mistrust like a person who never takes the blame for anything. They become the town crier to the rest of the team, as their predictable "It wasn't me" retorts often place them in a position of denial. As leaders (and we all are leaders), we must realize that mistakes will happen. We also must realize that sometimes we are going to make decisions (that are not necessarily mistakes) and people will disagree with them. These circumstances should be lauded instead of avoided, for they are what create and sustain the balance of a system.

Take initiative. If you do feel as though someone has defamed your reputation, you do have the right to solicit information regarding it. Obviously, do not go about this in an accusatory fashion. Gather your evidence and be willing to talk about it. Assume good intentions until proven otherwise; then forgive.

NOTE

1. Paul Zelinsky, *The Wheels on the Bus* (New York: Penguin, 1990).

SIXTEEN
I Do It for the Kids

Jennifer Tracy was a polished seventh grade English teacher, and someone who prided herself on being "a person of integrity." Today was her post conference with Mrs. Myers, the principal of Maple Junior High. Jennifer sat confidently across from Mrs. Myers. In being almost twice her age, Jennifer wondered what type of advice was forthcoming. A thorough administrator, Mrs. Myers reviewed the notes she had taken during her observation. Just as she was beginning the topic of instructional goal-setting, Jennifer interrupted.

"Mrs. Myers, I appreciate the time you have put into this meeting. And I understand that you have a job to do. But I don't teach for accolades or to please adults. I do it for the kids."

Mrs. Myers stopped in mid-sentence and just waited to see if Jennifer was going to say anything further. She did not.

Although Mrs. Myers tried to engage Jennifer in a conversation pertaining to her belief system, she could see her mind was set. At the conclusion of the meeting, both offered their customary pleasantries, and neither discussed the incident from that day forward.

Although not verbalized in quite the manner that Jennifer did, this situation is commonplace. Unfortunately, "I do it for the kids" is more than a cliché for some; it's a mantra! It serves to best the user from not only the discussion at hand but also the entire organization.

The linguistic breakdown speaks volumes for the intended and hidden meanings. First, the word *I* separates individuals from the team, as it positions the speaker at the center of the issue. Next, what we "do" often defines our purpose and provides the speaker with a false sense of worth. The "it" in this situation is flexible. Whatever the topic, "it" has it covered. Lastly, when we leverage the students in a disagreement, we create an ethical justification for our side of the argument.

For example, if Jennifer would have just concluded with "I don't teach for accolades," one may have been able to surmise (maybe) that her intent could have been positive in that she follows a righteous path toward justice (her own justice, but justice nonetheless). However, when she adds "I do it for the kids," she has drawn the traditional line in the sand between herself, her principal, and everyone else.

This tactic almost resembles a bully mentality, as it backs Mrs. Myers into a corner. Even dismissing the negative attitude about her age, Mrs. Myers's position has been questioned as being detrimental to the process of educating children. Of course Jennifer has a more direct line on impacting children on a daily basis. But to believe that each action, whether agreed on or not, does not have even the most subtle effect for children neglects an understanding of systems.

As discussed in previous chapters, each realm of the organization serves a specific role in the process of educating a child. Yet there are those whose tendency is to cast off others as inconvenient malingerers. In her statement, "I understand that you have a job to do," Jennifer undermines not only the tasks of Mrs. Myers but also the indirect impact her tasks are having on Jennifer's time.

Needless to say, "I do it for the kids" people are everywhere, and they do not have to be just teachers. There are principals, central office folks, and others who utilize the students as their personal platform for attaining what they feel is important. For example, there was once a principal who loathed central office. (I realize *loathed* is a pretty strong word, but in this instance, the assumption of disdain was warranted.) Part of the reason he felt ire toward the bosses was due to their constant "encroachment" on the schools. He believed that site-based management was to be taken literally. He was the principal; it was "his" school, and he felt that the principal was the person who should have complete autonomy on the decisions that would ultimately impact the people in the building.

The dynamic impact a principal makes on a school and achievement is considerable. That is not what is in question. In this particular situation, no one was asking the principal to give up the chair; however, even at the slightest hint from central office that another way might be possible, this person would begin his rant of "I am not interested in anything that is not for the kids."

What this person and others fail to realize is that every move (intended or not) impacts children. The entire notion of "for the kids" is moot. Adult issues, although on the surface they may seem confined to the adults, impact children. For instance, even though a teacher may not want to be sick, utilizing a sick day impacts the kids. Again, being sick was not intended "for" the kids, but the unintended consequences of the action carries effect. Now, the judgment of the act being positive, negative, or neutral can only be tried in the eyes of the beholder. Maybe the substitute teacher was awful or better or whatever.

Clichés stop candid debate on issues by rendering all other points invaluable to the speaker's position. Consider the principal in this scenario:

There was an issue over reading assessments going on in the Hoover School District. Sharon Pops, the principal of one of the elementary schools, was engaged in a debate over whether or not to incorporate a new formative assessment model into next year's planning. Sharon was vehemently opposed as it was taking time away from instruction. While debating, Charles Grover, the assistant superintendent of the district, noted that the formative assessments would be beneficial in being able to pinpoint curriculum deficiencies and teacher expertise.

On cue, Sharon turned to him and retorted, "Charles, in all honesty, I am not interested in the adult issues. We have to stay focused on the kids. That's our job. Instruction is at the heart of what we do, and we cannot afford to lose any more time." Sharon continued to declare that other assessments were already operational. She also was willing to "allow" someone to pilot the formatives as long as it was not in her building. Needless to say, the squeaky wheel drove the meeting and arrived at her ultimate destination — the assessments were parked until the following year.

Although she did not exactly say "I do it for the kids," you can see the thread of the cliché in her argument. The kids are most important; I am focused on them; therefore, you are not. The logic follows—I am focused on kids with my position; therefore, your position is not.

What Sharon and others fail to realize is that each side is "doing" for the students. Wanting to check curriculum is done for students. Wanting quality teachers is done for students. Yet the owner of "I do it for the kids" dismantles the other stances by challenging them on a perceived ethical basis, questioning one's moral purpose that gives the appearance of running contrary to the mission of the district. *If Sharon is for the kids, everyone else is—you got it—not.* And the fear of not being able to defend one's position against the perceived moral blusters of another are what keep many a voice quiet in the presence of such self-appointed righteousness.

PRACTICE ADVICE

See the "kids" in everything. As discussed, the students and the issues that surround them are in everything we do. We cannot allow ourselves to prioritize our arguments based on the notion that children will suffer if we do not follow a certain path. As stated previously, even the adult issues impact students. For example, just because a principal is demanding that a certain purchase order must be processed in a more timely fashion than others because it is "for the kids" does not mean that other purchase orders are not important to the organization. Nor does it give the right on behalf of the principal to bully the purchasing agent into moving said request up the priority list. We all do it for the kids; how we do it and its value on the system should be debated, not dictated by false jurisdiction.

Politely discuss the cliché with the user. When one travels with a user of this stance, the courageous approach would be to have a conversation. Try to point toward the hidden meaning of the cliché and, more importantly, how it makes you feel. Garner empathy on the part of the user prior to your next jaunt with them. If this person cannot temper the use of such an argument, be ready to either provide solid evidence for your position and how it supports children or dispute the notion that her position is the only one that does. Avoid the confrontation until all avenues of compromise have first been utilized.

Establish behavioral norms that refute the use of clichés. Establishing behavioral norms is a fantastic way to set the table when it comes to providing a safe environment for open discussion. Make the elimination of this, and other known clichés, as one of your must-dos. Ask folks to discuss openly their ideas without judgment of others. Or better yet, start with the antithesis of what you believe and locate all the positives in it prior to refuting its worth. In this fashion, one will be able to, at the very least, eliminate the moral façade that comes with using the kids as power.

Quick Think

Cling to your passions as if they were the air you breathe, for in a sense, they are just that.

SEVENTEEN

It Is What It Is

Much has been written recently about resiliency, grit factor, and growth model when it comes to the brain and the power of interactive dynamics.[1] Yet without recognizing and shifting habitual, stagnant verbal patterns, our self-perceptions, along with our capacity to learn, diminishes. Such was the case for Amir Shire.

Amir Shire was a musical wizard. In fact, there was no instrument he could not master. Be it the piano, drums, or trumpet, Amir was simply a natural. So when he decided to go into teaching music, no one was surprised. Through hard work and perseverance, Amir was able to secure his degree and found employment at Martine Academy, a fine private school just outside of the city.

Amir, in being the only K–12 music teacher at Martine, had extensive flexibility and curriculum control. However, one thing Amir did not have a say in was the song selection to be played at concerts. That duty was performed by Mrs. Muzzy, one of the board director's wives.

Secretly, Amir wished he could make a few suggestions for the list. The songs Mrs. Muzzy selected were of quality, but they did not really speak to the talent level of the group nor did any melody represent him as a person. (This is not to say that songs must represent the conductor, but one wouldn't be so bad.)

Amir's closest friends would razz him periodically. "How's the Wedding March coming along?" Amir would laugh and politely dismiss their jabs with a simple, "It is what it is." Unfortunately for Amir, it was just that for six-plus years.

Finally, during one of the planning sessions with Mrs. Muzzy, Amir's new assistant Rodger took some initiative and asked if it would be possible to play a Brazilian mantra, a song that was near and dear to Amir's heart. Although she was not rude, Mrs. Muzzy politely dismissed the idea because folks at Martine cherished traditions.

When discussing the situation with Rodger, Amir thanked him for his efforts, but repeated his patent line in an effort to indoctrinate him into the culture—it was what it was for a long time at Martine. Better to leave well enough alone.

"Clichés dominate void conversations. Too often, we utilize a cliché when the imbalance of power tips away from our favor. 'It is what it is' is one such platitude that reflects a feeble feeling."[2] Amir is not unlike many of us who succumb to the powers that be. These "powers" become the various mechanisms and circumstances that surround our daily excursions.

We have all probably utilized this cliché. In fact, maybe it's a stallion in our verbal stable. Yet, unlike the steeds that run free in Absecon, New Jersey, this cliché is powerful enough to end any would-be explorer's next trek. But why?

Nothing halts thought like the period. In other words, our imaginations can be more valuable than our ability to solve initial inquiries, for once we seal off access to the external, we confine ourselves (and our thinking) to the parameters that have traditionally existed. Hello to the Mrs. Muzzys of the world!

In not trying to make a judgment about Mrs. Muzzy or private schools or Brazilian mantras, traditions represent a conscious acceptance and perpetuation of a social norm. For instance, someone may enjoy visiting their favorite coffee house to secure their patented blend of bean. And if this person happens to order the same thing every day, does this make him less of a person?

People like what they like. It is difficult to fault them for that. True, learning is limited if one decides not to venture from the caramel mocha; however, this decision does not condemn the rest of the days' learning (or the taste of our favorite blend). Yet one of the greatest lessons we can ever try to instill in our students is resilience or the elasticity that forms from minds that are willing to bend. However, amid this mission, we unfortunately succumb to the same forces that can and do limit a person's capacity to exist beyond the present moment ("I can't do this!").

Life does not always permit us to plan our next change. Despite trying to be ahead of the curve, there are circumstances that limit our freedom to choose (boss, laws, etc.) without consequence. Nevertheless, what can be planned is our reaction to change and the feelings that are associated with variance.

In not straining to be overdramatic, desperate feelings bring despair, and nothing promotes the desolation more than phrases like "it is what it is." By yielding to an impenetrable control, this cliché presents the user in a powerless state. But it does not have to be this way. "Perhaps adding two words to this cliché could make all the difference not only in our attitude, but also in building conversations that can lead to positive change. 'It is what it is . . . for now' brings hope to a traditionally despondent situation."[3]

Furthermore, there are those who use this maxim as a way to cope with situations they cannot control. For instance, if your new boss decides that the staff is not permitted to wear jeans on Fridays anymore, a person can respond with "It is what it is" not out of anger, but more as a matter-of-fact statement. Nonetheless, this statement gives the appearance that this alteration will be eternal. (I hear Darth Vader saying, "It is what it is. No jeans!" as his voice reverberates down the hallway.)

The danger in using the cliché even to agree with present reality is that it fosters a false sense of time and impact. Who knows? Just as the new boss discouraged the jeans, perhaps the next one will enjoy a good pair of Levi's. Here, the idea of "for now" really builds an understanding that things can and do change and that's okay.

We must be cautious not to limit our potential to deal with change by creating short-term coping mechanisms that yield unsustainable realities. *Clichés are the brakes of thinking, and the stop signs on the road to dynamic dialogues.*

PRACTICE ADVICE

No one can make you feel the way you feel. Choosing is a process of free will. And one of the benefits of having access to a litany of emotions is our ability to experience them all. Feelings of despair occur when we fail to see that ultimately power resides in us all. Even if a situation is so untenable that we feel we can no longer work within its parameters, there still exists a choice on how to approach the desired outcome. In simple terms, we are not forced to remain in despondent situations. Misery loves company, but nothing breathes life into a gathering like a positive outlook. Be the person who dares to dream the impossible.

Help break the habit. When a person states, "It is what it is," politely see if you can add the words "for now" behind the cliché. Start to build others' capacity for growth by identifying the root of the convention. Now, please keep in mind that some folks may not be open to this type of thinking. Likewise, others may take offense to you trying to "correct" them. Here is where tact plays a huge part in the delivery and adherence to the message. Remember the golden rule and tread softly . . . but purposely.

Teach resolve to the students. Ultimately, the lessons we employ are only as good as our ability to model their consistent approach. The more we can assist our students in taking control of their feelings toward change (while modeling similar actions in our own lives), the better the chance of impact. They may listen well, but will always witness more with mighty eyes.

NOTES

1. A. L. Duckworth, C. Peterson, M. D. Matthews, and D. R. Kelly, "Grit: Perseverance and Passion for Long-Term Goals," *Journal of Personality and Social Psychology* 92, no. 6 (June 2007): 1087–1101.

2. A. Barber, *The Hidden Principalship: A Practical Guide for New and Experienced Principals* (Lanham, MD: Rowman & Littlefield, 2013).

3. Ibid.

EIGHTEEN

All I Do for This Place

Gene Valente was a high school curriculum coach in the Kingways School District. Although he did not have a typical teaching schedule, curriculum coaches were still under the teachers' contract. Gene had volunteered for this position some three years ago when the school board decided it needed to enhance professional development without adding days to the contract or diminishing instruction for students.

Gene was a whiz with instruction. He was assisting many teachers with professional practice, and he really felt that he was making a difference. Lately, the job had shifted. With the new teacher-evaluation system, everyone seemed like they needed to take on added responsibilities. Gene was no exception.

With each passing day, Gene seemed to be moving in different directions, but finally he really found his stride again. Although he did not particularly agree with every aspect of the new system, he became a huge resource for the district. In fact, he even was the lead presenter at the public board meeting to describe the system. Things were going well, and as fate would have it, more good news followed.

Kingsway High School was going to be hiring a new assistant principal. Gene, having his administrative degree, never really thought he would leave the classroom; however, with this new position and the success that he was having, he decided that it might be time to give it a try. Furthermore, many staff members were asking him to apply. Even the outgoing assistant principal told him he would be good. High praise from a former mentor.

Gene applied for the position and had what he believed were amazing interviews. As the hiring commenced, Gene was confident. Truth be told, he would stop by the exiting principal's office and imagine his family pictures hanging on the walls. Exciting stuff!

Unfortunately for Gene, the hiring committee selected an outside candidate who had a boatload of experience when it came to scheduling (not one of Gene's strong suits). Gene was none too happy with the results.

Acknowledging his lack of scheduling experience, Gene was mystified with the decision. He had learned the new teacher-evaluation system in a flash. He certainly could have picked up scheduling, especially being a former trigonometry teacher.

As time went on, Gene grew bitter. He did his job, but started to cut out the "extra" effort. Soon, even his regular work became mundane. Gene was even heard griping to other staff members that he was tired of giving so much to a system that did not give back.

It is not farfetched to read this situation and picture someone who has lived it. There are literally thousands of Genes who give a fantastic effort at their current job and look to someday secure the next one (promotion). And like Gene, sometimes those next ones find their way into the hands of others—an unfortunate situation, but one of reality in finite conditions.

Folks can be disappointed when the next job does not pan out. We are all human beings, and sometimes our desires surpass reality. In other words, the feelings of anticipated glory can place us in a vulnerable position if and when the situation does not come to exist.

Now, despite the possibility for letdown, we cannot avoid risk. On the contrary, we need not "go gentle into that good night" to secure life's opportunities.[1] Yet we must also understand that the potential for failure does exist if and when we decide to try.

Gene took a risk, an amazing step, and one that should be appreciated despite the outcome. However, Gene unfortunately allowed his sense of self to soar, as his current success seemed to be pointing in the direction of victory. No one can fault him for thinking he was going to get the job or his disappointment thereafter. However, it was his next reaction that causes the greatest concern.

Although this may seem unkind, as educators, we rent with no option to buy. And some would even argue that leasing is a thing of the past. We cannot set our modus operandi to overvalue our worth in a system that continues to exist even when we do not. In simple terms, although Gene could probably have completed the tasks of an assistant principal, someone else could too, thus setting up a situation where Gene did not have the only golden ticket for entrance into the factory.[2]

This situation occurs every day in every district across the universe. For instance, there was a principal who had an amazing run. She assisted in raising the student achievement scores, assisted in lowering the achievement gap between students, and helped to build a positive culture to where teachers requested to work in the building.

Now, the time came for her departure, and predictably, there were some that mourned the loss. Yet, as she drove out of the parking lot for the last time as the principal, she noticed something interesting. No one was chaining the doors to the school. In other words, when she did not show up to school on the next day, the school would still be opened. Students and teachers would be there. Learning would occur and life would go on. Despite all of the pronounced work and the decade of service to this school, life would go on . . . without her.

This last tale is not meant to cause sadness but to remind us about how systems function. *Picture the school system as an escalator.* We step on at a certain place with the hope of exiting a little higher than we came in. That is the impact we desire for our students and ourselves—to make that positive difference. Yet we must understand that as we exit the staircase, others step on with their hope of reaching new pinnacles. Such is the cycle of systems.

To truly survive the system, we cannot limit our perspective to just ourselves. We need to cherish the times we have in these jobs; we cannot look on these jobs as grudges, but as gifts. Yes, we do for the school, but we also do for ourselves as well.

Thankfully, Gene did see the error in his thinking. Although it took a few years to figure it out, he always believed in the adage "better late than never." That's my boy!

PRACTICE ADVICE

True character resides in places that are immune to ego. Of course it is perfectly satisfactory to be upset when the fruits of our labor do not yield the anticipated results for future prosperity. Yet do not forget the ones who are impacted in a positive manner just by doing what we are supposed to do. If the accolades come, that's amazing. But do not perform tasks with the hope that others will recognize and reward them. Do what needs to be done because it will serve the greater good. This way, whether or not the praise hits our ears, we can feel secure that we have given, that we have mattered beyond the lighted stage of someone else's drama.

Assist others in the quest to serve without pretense. This is not to say that you need to be forceful in this plight. If you should happen to hear someone utter those famous words, at a later time, try to converse with them about the situation and how this line of thinking can damage one's positive core. Obviously, we should not take a preacher approach to this circumstance. Help others explore their feelings and locate the balance that allows us to exist and thrive in a system immersed in emotion.

Teach your students this skill. Ultimately, the lessons we replicate are the ones that stick! Demonstrate a selfless stance with your students. Talk about doing a job the right way (not for the next one). Help them see that actions tied to self-motivation have a better chance of sustaining than those that are accomplished for external outcomes. If you model, they will follow.

NOTES

1. Dylan Thomas, *Do Not Go Gentle into That Good Night* (New York: Richard Reynolds & John Stone, 1951).
2. Roald Dahl, *Charlie and the Chocolate Factory* (New York: Alfred A. Knopf, 1964).

Quick Think

The search for Nirvana must start with a belief that one exists.

NINETEEN
The Dance of the Lemons

Heidi Thomas sat quietly for the first hour. In being the new principal of Weber Elementary School, she knew enough to allow her listening to do her speaking, especially during her maiden voyage at the district-level staffing meeting.

However, Heidi did have experience with staffing in the Clover School District. Being a former teacher in the district for fifteen years and now an administrator, she knew all too well the feeling in the staff at this time of year. Transfer season was stressful, especially for the folks on the front line who sat helplessly awaiting word whether or not their "cheese would be moved."[1]

In fact, Heidi had firsthand experience in transfers, for during her fourth year of employment, she was transferred from Gladwyne Elementary to Oaks. It was a very trying time to say the least. It is difficult to leave your friends and students, especially when so many positive bonds have been set. Nonetheless, Heidi did what she was supposed to do and did it with class.

Interestingly, the very principal who "transferred" her to Oaks turned out to be her mentor principal, Dr. Louise Duvet. And now, Dr. Duvet sat directly across from her during the staffing meeting. Although Dr. Duvet had somewhat prepped Heidi for the meeting, the good doctor's final comments were what resonated with Heidi: "All is fair in love and staffing."

The staffing meeting moved quickly. Principals jostled for position. Assistant superintendent Linda Bronstein did her best to try and squash would-be bullies by allowing each person to speak on each topic. This made for a long meeting, but certainly a necessary tactic.

Staffing is based on enrollment, offerings, and desired class size. In Heidi's building, student enrollment was on the rise; therefore, Heidi was in need of staffing. Unfortunately, this was not always the most secure position (needing staff during this meeting).

Just as student enrollment may be rising at one building, another school may have the complete opposite situation occurring. Such was the case for Dr. Du-

vet's school. Dr. Duvet needed to transfer one staff member, as her numbers simply could not support keeping the position.

Finally, it was time to focus on Weber Elementary. In knowing that Heidi needed staffing, Dr. Duvet turned her attention to Heidi and blurted out three names from which she could select. Heidi was a bit unnerved. "Are we not going to discuss this situation? I thought I would receive a hire." She asked.

The rest of the room snickered. Someone even whispered, "Rookie." Dr. Bronstein did her best to explain that due to the contract, everyone needed to keep their job. In which case, transfers were necessary to attain balance. Heidi understood.

Heidi turned to Dr. Duvet, who was smiling and shaking her head as if to say, "Well?" Heidi then said, "Louise, I do not know these people. So just pick one for me."

At that moment, another principal started to make beeping noises as if a truck was backing up. Dr. Bronstein silenced the crowd again and awaited Dr. Duvet's selection. She picked the second one in the series.

As the meeting concluded, Heidi got the feeling there was a tremendous amount of unspoken conversation that she missed during her exchange with Dr. Duvet. In fact, as she was walking to her car, Mary, a long-time principal of another school, politely gave her a pat on the back and said, "Welcome." As it turns out, Heidi's new staff member was not a shining star. Such was the method and madness of the Dance of the Lemons.

Sadly, this story is not fabricated. Although the names have been changed, the entire manuscript was almost taken word for word. The "dance" is alive, and many teachers and administrators know all too well the movement and motion that goes into its rhythm.

The Dance of the Lemons cliché can be linked to automobiles. A *lemon* is a term we use to tag a car that is faulty. We all can probably picture a slick used-car salesman getting ready to do his best Houdini sleight of hand on an unsuspecting client. Nowadays, these types of shysters are put into check with the advent of the internet and Carfax reports. Yet, if we can gather so much data on a car's condition in an instant, why would we not be able to do the same for teachers? Could Heidi have asked to see her potential teacher's Carfax?

Of course, teacher evaluation systems provide data on teacher performance and at many staffing meetings, these reports are readily available. However, very rarely do they tell the whole story. There are many reasons why these reports are void of critical information, but the most important piece of information has to do with something that we label as "shining."

Shining occurs when a person does her best to promote the appearance of a person without exposing the person's weakness to others. Picture the old adage "she has a great personality." Can you begin to develop an understanding that the person's personality might not be the focus?

Why do people shine others? Sometimes people believe the system forces us to move problems instead of dealing with them. In schools these days, we blame teacher-evaluation systems and unions. We blame administrative agreements, the lawyers, and the lack of time, resources, and support to do the hard work necessary to handle people issues. Hogwash!

This type of thinking is a hoax! One of the biggest fabrications in schools today is that people cannot manage other people when it comes to performance. Admittedly, it is not an easy proposition. And certainly in the business world, it becomes a much easier road to travel in terms of improvement plans or dismissals. Yet to use the excuses to justify the lack of action is shifty. Most times, people shine others because it is easier. (I do realize there are times in terms of legal settlements and such where it is necessary to give a generic recommendation; the instances I am referring to do not include specific occasions of necessary shining.)

Undeniably, there are also times when a "fresh start" for a person can be a great opportunity for someone to regain their stride; likewise, there are times when a person is really needed in another part of the organization, and therefore, a transfer is necessary. In other words, please do not look at every transfer as a lemon twist. There are legitimate reasons for movement.

Despite all of the specifics of this example, the true misstep occurs in the lack of honest conversation between Dr. Duvet and Heidi. In fact, the lack of discussion on the part of all of the administrators is concerning. The "one-up" attitude and action on the part of Dr. Duvet and the acceptance on the part of the group demonstrate the lack of genuine concern each has for the good outside of their domain. But what would create such a situation, whereby we would feel we need to hide in the shadows . . . even with our own mentee?

Certainly, the pressure can get to everyone. And surely it becomes easy to focus solely on our own situation, especially when accountability is high and resources are limited. However, notwithstanding such situations, we must fight against the burden to raise ourselves at the expense of others.

The only way the *Dance of the Lemons* will cease to exist is if we turn off the manufactured melody and begin to talk to one another about difficult topics. It is only in our honesty that we can truly find our stride and assist others and ourselves to truly shine!

PRACTICE ADVICE

The dance is everywhere; hear it and react. The Dance of the Lemons exists on all levels of the organization. Be it in the classroom or the offices, those who fail to communicate honestly and openly with others continue to shuffle the deck on needed conversations. Certainly, there are times when discretion is needed. But those that "play nice" instead of having difficult conversations create an atmosphere of suspicion.

Do not judge the moved. Again, transfers happen for many reasons and with many people. Try hard not to bring judgment against this person when the facts of the situation are not known. (Recall the warnings of conspiracy.) Likewise, even if a person was moved to gather a fresh start, that is exactly what we should afford him or her. We must allow a person the benefit of shedding all of the past negatives for a chance to create a new legacy. This undercurrent of "he must have done something wrong because he was transferred" really needs to stop. Do your best to put this conspiracy to rest.

If you are being transferred, go with a rising spirit. Although this is not easy to do, if you should happen to be transferred, do your best to see every change as an opportunity to gather new experiences. Maybe you will find your best friend, your wife or husband, your greatest educational breakthrough. The possibilities are endless so long as we do not diminish our own potential.

Note: Did you notice how Dr. Duvet selected the second person in the line of three? What does that tell you about her strategy? Pretty disingenuous! Important to mention is that the new superintendent changed the entire process the following year, and thankfully, honest conversations are now occurring.

NOTE

1. Spencer Johnson, *Who Moved My Cheese?: An Amazing Way to Deal with Change in Your Work and in Your Life* (New York: Putnam, 1998).

IV

Practical Approaches

TWENTY

Culture Builders

A "culture builder" is a hands-on idea that can be used immediately. Culture builders range from concise strategies for success with people to simple actions to take in situations.

FOR TEACHERS

Be Where You Are Supposed to Be When You Are Supposed to Be There

Mrs. Harley was the type of teacher who expected students to have their materials. She was not a "mean" teacher, but certainly demanded a level of responsibility from her twelfth grade students. Her famous line, "These are young adults; in the real world, they won't be able to slide by" meshed perfectly with her belief system.

However, despite Mrs. Harley's student stance, she could never seem to follow her own counsel. She was late for meetings, was late with her grades, and barely showed up to any of her extra duty assignments. Claiming she was "just swamped" left her colleagues tired, as her assertions of being busy diminished everyone else's contributions. Likewise, her principal was also becoming weary of her antics. Despite being a quality instructor, her actions in "the real world" were less than desirable.

Too often, it becomes easy for us to assume a "do as I say not as I do" approach to life. This is not to say we are malicious in our intent. Nevertheless, the lack of attention to our individual responsibilities creates a negative impression of who we are and diminishes the value of our contribution to the organization. Furthermore, when we make claims about the real world and then do not heed those same warnings, we build a reputation of being a hypocrite.

The advice for this situation is very simple: Be where you are supposed to be when you are supposed to be there. There's no need to expand on this situation, as failure to adhere to this truism will create distance between you and the principal and craft a foundation for dissention and unrest with your colleagues. As Nike states, "Just do it."

Find the Facts — Limit the Whisper

Our brains want to make connections. Schemas want to be linked and filed; however, we must fight against the tendency to accept gossip as gospel. For busy people, this motto is easier said than done, as connections to items that do not directly impact us (gossip about others) sometimes are easily dismissed. However, even the simplest of stories can define a person's reputation in our brains.

For example, if someone is being accused of stealing, and we do not have the time or access to locate evidence, we must make a conscious decision not to accept the accusation as truth until the situation has come to resolution. Although this advice might seem like a no-brainer, many problems with school morale can be linked to gossip and the impact it has on a person's character (even without that person having knowledge of the initial gossip).

In addition, those that blather on eventually ostracize themselves as people that cannot be trusted. Like the damage that goes undetected to the recipient of the gossip, the gossiper also collects baggage for his part in the process.

The best bet is to avoid the prattle that accompanies a mind lacking substance. If someone is continually spreading rubbish about, you have the right (politely) to let him or her know that this type of behavior is not appreciated. If we reap what we sow, we must grow what we know — not what we think might be.

Propose Possible Solutions

How do you feel when a student forgets a pencil? If you were most folks, you probably have a huge container of them somewhere in the classroom, as best practice would tell us not to quibble over the small issues. However, if you have told the students time and time again that if they forget a pencil they can borrow one without asking, the myriad of "Can I get a pencil" requests might become a bit unnerving.

Now take this concept and think about the principal. These folks deal with issues all day long. Sure, we all have issues, but adult issues can be a bit more intricate, as they tend to have impact for both teachers and their students. With that being said, one of the most proactive strategies a teacher (or any staff member) can possess is the ability to bring possible solutions to a problem.

Of course there will be times when the issue is enormous, and more resources will be necessary to amend the situation. Yet those who at least have demonstrated and articulated some thought behind even a starting place gain credibility, unlike those who complain things are awry and wait for someone to do something, and then complain on how the snag was mended.

The world has way too many Monday-morning quarterbacks. Don't be one of them. Enter the game at its zenith. Take a risk and share what you know. Great ideas start with the idea to start . . . and a pencil.

When You Are Sick, Call Early

Covering absences in the building has to be one of the most stressful duties ever created in schools. Seriously! Ensuring that each class has a certified adult present to deliver instruction and maintain safety is no joke. Many gray hairs have been sprouted by the process of coverages, and nothing throws a wrench into the plan like the late sick call.

Clearly, if a person wakes up ill and has no resolve but to call, there is nothing wrong with this practice. However, if you truly know you will be (*cough, cough*) taking a sick day, then please do us all a favor and let the office know as soon as you can. Likewise, if you are not sick, but are having another issue that will hinder your ability to be on time, please make that appeal in a timely manner as well.

Furthermore, if you are the habitual offender of the late sick call, please understand that the office can start to request documentation for proof. Similarly, note that your legacy may start to be defined by this situation as opposed to the wonderful work you do in the classroom. Being professional is paramount in building positive culture that lasts.

So if you are sick, take your benefit. Get well. Rest. Let the office know as soon as possible.

Remember Your Primary Function

Primary function (PF) is a term that is used to define one's most critical responsibility to the success of the school. For example, if the head custodian is an excellent math tutor and assists students after school each day but fails to empty the trash cans because he is busy tutoring, his PF would be in the negative. Although it would be wonderful to provide the extra support for students, neglecting our primary responsibilities to the organization in the name of auxiliary ones breaks down the effectiveness of the system.

Unfortunately, this type of situation occurs regularly. Although most times it is not intentional, coaches and sponsors sometimes have such a passion for their particular event that they sometimes place their subject

(PF) on the backburner, especially during the height of their season (playoffs, concerts, etc.).

As the complaints start to roll in, administrators are forced to address the topic with the sponsors, and inevitably, a negative feel is created on behalf of the sponsor. In simple terms, the sponsor feels squeezed because of time, pressure, and so on. This type of situation can often lead to an "All I do for this place" circumstance.

One of the best ways to counter this situation is to always remember that your primary function has to be your focus . . . even during the playoffs. If you are the eleventh grade math instructor and also the class advisor, you must find a way to balance the tasks so that your math students get the best instruction possible.

FOR ADMINISTRATORS

Know the Staff

If "Know thy self" is one of the greatest attributes we can have in leadership, a close second would definitely be "Know the staff." As we have discussed in almost every chapter, our connection to the people in our organization along with our genuine passion for their success is what breathes life into our worlds.

One of the most successful texts ever written on the topic of human interactions and business is Dale Carnegie's *How to Win Friends and Influence People*. Of the many notable strategies Dale discusses, one of the most memorable has to do with man's best friend.[1]

To summarize, Dale believed leaders could learn a great deal from dogs, for just as they are genuinely excited to see us (wagging their tail), we must be that passionate about people in our lives. In taking this idea a step further, we must acknowledge the belief that the only secure thing in life is that we are all insecure. In believing each of us craves connection, what could be better than to know that you have someone in your corner no matter the circumstance?

When leaders take the time to genuinely understand the staff, to withhold judgment from their shortcomings and look for opportunities to serve, they create a culture of positive appeal. The first step in realizing this mission is to always place the human beings above the tasks of the building. Help people to define their purpose and passions. Build opportunities for them to explore their interests and motivations. Laugh, cry, and experience life with them. This is leadership!

Build the Dimmer Switch

Sometimes leaders place a tremendous burden on themselves to be the authority of each circumstance. For example, just because the principal may have a learned opinion on which textbook series to utilize does not mean that she should automatically offer her beliefs prior to the staff's investigation on the topic. Allowing a process to commence and securing all perspectives provides a better opportunity for attaining a more supported position. Likewise, we increase internal motivation when we provide a forum for people's belief systems to be heard.

Sometimes leaders see their role as providing light to darkness. In other words, leaders often believe that their job is to provide the answers to those who do not have them. However, consider what happens to people when they have been in a dark room and someone quickly turns the lights on. Our first reaction to this occurrence is to squint and turn away from the source of the light.

Great leaders see one of the most critical components of leadership as devising systems that allow folks to investigate, negotiate, and create opportunities based on human interaction. In this sense, they do not position themselves as technical, topical experts, but look to establish a system for others to try what works for them.

In your next circumstance, instead of flipping the lights up and blinding people with your position or possible solution, try to build a process that allows people to find their own light switch and then make sure the switch is on a dimmer so they can adjust the light to their eyes in accordance to their differentiated perspective. This may seem like a fruitless task, and one that can be avoided, but always remember decisions based on power have a greater chance of succeeding than those based on rank.

Be a Straight Shooter

There was once a teacher who used to say, "I tell it like it is." In realizing that "like it is" was a biased position based on the opinion and circumstance surrounding her issue, the general premise still resonates. She valued brevity and folks who do not beat around the bush.

In school systems, there can be a tendency to be politically correct to the detriment of the relationships within. People sometimes will not inform a colleague about a situation either for fear of alienating themselves from the colleague or simply because "that is their business."

As administrators, there are many times when we must inform people of all types of situations and decisions. And although we should be mindful of the person's well-being, the worst thing we can do is play games when it comes to information. Those who talk around the issue instead of talking directly create an environment of skepticism. Just as the little boy who cried wolf, administrators who talk in tongue lose their credibility when they finally need to be direct with staff members.

In addition, leaders who talk too much and fail to participate in active-listening strategies are doomed to be blathering fools in the eyes of their staff. These folks unfortunately demonstrate their lack of confidence in their overabundance of chatter. The constant barrage of verbal nonsense nibbles a staff to the core, as members start to see this person as someone who cannot be trusted because he or she cannot keep her mouth tight.

Listen more, and when you need to speak, be polite and be direct.

Limit the Jokes

John Turner was an elementary principal who loved to joke around with the staff. Unfortunately, his type of jokes did not start off with "knock knock." John's jokes were not jokes at all but were reminders of who was in charge. Be it "I could fit your wallet into mine" or "I get paid to watch the game," his little jabs felt like right hooks to the embattled staff whose sole desire was for him to just do his job without the pageantry.

Sometimes people in leadership positions feel the need to keep folks "under their thumb" when it comes to the power issues of the building. Oftentimes, these situations are created by a lack of technical knowledge on the part of the leader.

For instance, John's greatest jests usually occurred during literacy meetings. In being a former math teacher, John did not have the expertise in literacy. So instead of learning more about the subject, his tack was to make sure everyone knew that despite his knowledge deficit, he was in charge as noted by "the big principal name plate that hangs on the office door."

Bully administrators do not last, as eventually they are usually taken out by someone with bigger name plates. Do yourself and the staff a favor and limit the jokes. This is not to say that you cannot have a sense of humor when it comes to the job. But be wary of the subtle (they are not really that subtle) shots that folks take to flex their muscles in social situations.

Remember, everyone knows who the principal is. The need to boast should be suppressed to create a more collegial environment for all.

Be Visible

If you ask teachers to tally the traits of a fantastic administrator, being visible would have to be a close second to being supportive. As the years have gone by, the idea of being visible has taken on a different connotation than just being seen. Part of the reasons has to do with the structure of schools and the research surrounding safety.

Principals who are visible *and active* have the ability to be proactive in situations where others may be unaware of the goings on in a particular setting. Many a fight has been stopped prior to the first punch being thrown simply by having an adult present in the environment. For this and other reasons, school personnel want to increase their adult supervision.

Yet despite the obvious benefit of the principal helping to halt potential situations, being visible and active lets the staff know that you are all in this together. Principals that sit in their office all day garner a reputation for being lazy, even if they are working on projects. As the leaders of the building, administrators must demonstrate a tireless effort when it comes to being "in the moment" for the staff and students.

So stop by classrooms. Get your hands dirty in a lab activity. Run a lunchtime basketball tournament on rainy days. Whatever you can do to support the events of the building in a physical way will go a long way in bridging any potential gaps that may exist in the morale.

Plus, what better way to connect with students than to participate in a science lab or sponsor a lunch activity? Just be sure not to forget about your primary functions, as others may start to notice if you are playing basketball in the gym with the students and not attending to other critical areas.

NOTE

1. Dale Carnegie, *How to Win Friends and Influence People* (New York: Pocket Books, 1936).

TWENTY-ONE

Culture Busters

A "culture buster" is a situation or tactic that should be avoided at all costs. Culture busters erode the fabric of the team by creating imbalance to the system or to power structures.

FOR TEACHERS

Promoting Conspiracy

How do you feel when someone says, "Those who can do, and those who cannot teach"? Obviously, the person who is making such a statement has never had to lesson plan to standards or manage a classroom with different learning styles and behavior tendencies. Needless to say, this person's lack of knowledge as to what teachers do day in and day out is only matched by their inability to understand the dynamic components of human beings and learning.

Nonetheless, the statement holds with it power, for the more times it is repeated by this person and others, the more damage it does to the foundation of teaching and the folks who dedicate their lives to its mission.

Conspiracies erode the fabric of positive environments by creating misperception. Conspiracies alienate the user and the accused by positioning the user (the one starting or prolonging the conspiracy) in an elevated power status. In other words, the person spreading the conspiracy assumed a false sense of power over the topic (the person) by controlling the flow of information (true or otherwise).

We all have heard the saying, "If you do not have anything nice to say. . . ." What a wonderful world it would be if we could actually follow this idea, especially when it comes to gossip. Do your best to limit the perpetual game of tag that occurs each time we relay a rumor without facts. (We may never be able to stop the jealousy that sometimes hinders our profession, but limiting our participation in the gossip game will go a long way in establishing a positive climate.)

Public Ridicule

William Kulak could not understand why his principal was so upset with him. Dr. James had always had an open-door policy concerning various factors in the building. Be it leadership team summits, curriculum development sessions, or simple planning meetings, Dr. James wanted feedback. In knowing this to be the case, William wondered why this time his comments caused so much ire.

During yesterday's faculty meeting, Dr. James was reviewing the new safety procedures for the building. William, in being very meticulous in his subject and life, located several mistakes within the presentation and did his best to point out those errors so that each member of the staff could make the changes to their manuals.

The staff really seemed to appreciate William's attention to detail, as noted by their "good eyes" comments. However, Dr. James did not have the same reaction. In fact, he seemed aggravated with William. Almost mad. Wouldn't he want the manuals to be correct?

Obviously, every administrator would want the handbooks to have the correct information in them, especially when lives are at stake. However, we must remember our insecurities as it relates to public forums. Just as a teacher would not want a student to constantly interrupt them in a given lesson, I am sure Dr. James was feeling embarrassed each time William's hand went up.

Should Dr. James have had the book edited? Of course! Likewise, he could have stated that he needed everyone's eyes on the manual, thus empowering folks to find mistakes without undermining his efforts. However, he did not.

Can you correct someone's thinking? Yes, but it may be best to do it in a more private setting.

Grading Papers during Meetings

If there ever was a more observable "do as I say not as I do" in education, it might be embodied in this particular topic. We all know how it feels when a student is working on another teacher's assignment during our class. We may have compassion for the immediacy of the need; however, the underlying message (this subject is more important than yours) creates a distance between us, the student, and sometimes the other teacher. Such a gap can cause great harm to not only our relationships but the student's grades as well.

Now fast forward to the faculty meeting. Inevitably, there is always one teacher who feels the need to grade papers during it. This person demonstrates not only poor judgment but also the same disrespect that the student creates in the classroom. And what happens? The relationship between the administrator and the teacher widens. Plus, other folks on the staff inevitably await the confrontation or lack thereof. Either way, negative reigns.

Just as a teacher can stop a student from working on another assignment, a principal can take it upon herself to hinder the grading too. Yet this type of reactive nature brings with it ill will. Do yourself, your colleagues, and your principal a huge favor: don't grade papers at meetings. Do your best to be an active listener and demonstrate the respect that you would want from your audience.

Being a professional requires us to sometimes place the needs of others in front of our own. Thank you in advance for your cooperation.

Say You Can When You Cannot

There was this guy I knew years ago who would always tell his friends he was going to go out with them but never did. Be it going to a ball game, attending a concert, or simply hanging out at someone's house, this person was notorious for telling everyone he would "meet them there" only to have his absence (and potential excuses) noticed. As time went by, this person's invitations started to wane. In fact, he rarely got called to do anything. Bummer.

People can and do come up with the craziest justifications to cover potential problems. From "the dog ate my homework" to "I was feeling under the weather," excuses abound in desperate situations. Too often, the people who make excuses are either too busy or sincerely do not want to hurt someone by saying no.

We all know the harm that comes from lying and this form of excuse borders on this pretext. As with a bandage, it is better to take it off with the first swipe than to continue to inch it off piece by piece. Some would say that bad news should come "early and often." Although this may seem like a negative situation, having a more direct approach to saying no protects relationships from huge letdowns.

If you are unable to accomplish a certain task or attend a certain event, just say it. If the person is truly a friend, he or she will understand. Conjuring figments of our imagination to fulfill the next white lie only serves to lengthen the distance between ourselves and our peers. If you cannot do something, simply say you cannot and move on.

Not Seeing the Gray

Of all of the colors in the rainbow, maybe the most important one for an educator is the color gray. Aside from its simplistic reverence or stately charm, the color gray also serves as a metaphor for understanding human interactions.

As mentioned, human beings are dynamic creatures, and our existence is documented in the trials and tribulations of various ideas. Be it selecting a new social studies curriculum or selecting a restaurant for dinner, technical answers (the correct ones) do not exist when we add free will and choice to circumstance. In knowing that culture and context have its place in every decision that is debated, the right answers are determined by consensus instead of conquest.

Teachers who have the ability to see their beliefs but also the ones of others who may be in direct opposition to them have a far better chance at succeeding in the system than those that cannot bend. People who are too black and white pigeonhole their thoughts, which in turn, compromises their ability to see choice and understand the balance of power.

Control is only afforded when the stakeholders agree to a value system that acts as a balance to the system. For instance, a child not motivated by grades may not be spurred to action by the threat of a zero. Those who cannot see the gray in their classrooms, hallways, and schools most times end up seeing green in envy, red in anger, and blue in despair.

Sometimes perfect isn't always right!

FOR ADMINISTRATORS

Making Promises to Appease Conflict

Tyler Reus was a compassionate human being who wanted the best for people. So when he became an assistant principal, he was so excited to finally be in a position where he felt like he could make a huge impact on the school. And he certainly did the minute he processed his first referral.

Tyler, in wanting to let Mrs. Griggs know that she had his support, let her know that he was going to suspend Kirk Hester from her class because of his insubordination. Unfortunately, he had told her this prior to meeting with Kirk. Once he had the contact meeting with him, Tyler noticed some inconsistencies with the referral. In not wanting to upset Kirk's father, who was known to be a handful, he gave Kirk a warning and sent him on his way.

As one could imagine, Mrs. Griggs was none too happy with his decisions. In wanting her to be "happy" again, he promised her if Kirk even breathed wrong, he would suspend him.

Know anybody like this? This type of "let's make a deal" mentality creates such an imbalance in a system that needs structure. Administrators who waver on decisions to appease those who are in front of them doom the culture of the building by abolishing fact for less friction. In turn, the nonaction only serves to create more conflict at a deeper degree, thus undermining the tenets of impartiality.

Administrators can make determinations and recommendations based on an investigative procedure and fact. But to make decisions based on the reactions of others simply won't do. Again, if the answer is no, then say no.

Giving a General Warning

We have all received one of these emails:

> Good morning everyone,
>   It has come to my attention that several members of our staff are still arriving late to school. As stated in last month's faculty meeting, our work day starts at 7:30 a.m. We cannot continue to arrive late to school, as this practice is both violating the contract and also causing a morale problem for those who arrive on time!!!! Thank you for your compliance.
>
> Mr. Thomas Morris

How do you feel reading this email? Now imagine how your staff feels. Tom had addressed the issue in a previous faculty meeting and instead of having the personal conversation (and more difficult one), he opted to again use a general warning. Come on, Tom!

Look—everyone knows when someone is coming in late, leaving early, skipping their duty, and so on. Too often, administrators veil behind the general warnings when best practice would be to put the laptop down and stand in the hallway at 7:25 a.m. And if someone is late, let them know. Define the expectations with respect, dignity, and a smidgen of firmness.

As stated before, principals need to keep the balance. This tenet will also ask us to administer between the people who do what they are supposed to do and those who do not. Please, please, please do not take the easy way out. Better to be a little uncomfortable now than to try and fix a culture that is stained by our inability to do the tough work.[1]

Ducking the Difficult Conversations

We have all faced adversity at one time or another in our lives. Maybe at work or in a social setting, these ordeals bring with them a host of challenges, and one task that sometimes accompanies potential conflict is having the difficult conversation.

Although some folks will say that being able to chat with someone about troublesome issues is innate, we must believe that this skill can be improved. Likewise, our ability to realize that a potential conversation is on the horizon can and does assist in planning for and delivering on the next exchange.

For example, if you had a teacher who you believed was not pulling his weight as the professional instructor, prior to having a life-altering notification, at the very least a mini-conversation should have commenced to let him know his current status. We call this practice "the meeting before the meeting" and it has assisted many folks in impacting change.

Those who sidestep difficult dialogue or mince words to hint at hidden meanings create a powerless feeling for those on the receiving end of the discussion. When these folks could be digesting and planning a new course of action for potential problems, they are compressed into translating cryptic jargon.

When we have facts on our side, it takes nothing to be compassionate when giving news. If we look on this responsibility as a chance to assist someone in becoming better, then having the tough talk is no longer a nicety but a necessity for building capacity in our people.

Going to Committee When the Decision Is Already Made

Rocky Schullery was the assistant superintendent in the Sather County School District. His work with curriculum, instruction, and assessment was impeccable, as he had a keen ability to foster a collaborative spirit among the teams of teachers. Ironically, in being so collaborative with his teachers, the principals in the district were always flabbergasted by how Rocky treated them.

Rocky was a committee man. He loved the dialogue and process that was associated with gathering stakeholders together for a common purpose. Unfortunately, Sather County schools, along with the rest of the state schools, were being bombarded by the state's education department. Many mandates were being funneled to the schools, all of which were both unfunded and specific in their charge.

Despite the state's assault on the schools, Rocky continued to follow his practice of having committees to discuss the issues. The principals, who used to appreciate Rocky's style, now grimaced every time they saw an email from him. Another committee, another decision that was already known. The practice was getting tired to say the least.

Have you ever been on a committee where you know the decision is already made? Talk about a lack of respect for people's time. Certainly, Rocky could pull folks together to discuss and brainstorm on how items would be addressed, but to facilitate committees when decisions have been determined undermines intelligence and minimizes morale.

If you (or another entity) have to make a decision, then just make it. Do not play the "buy-in" game. Sure, it is best to make command decisions in crisis, and negotiate outcomes in peaceful times, but if a decision has already been made, masking its inception only destroys potential collaboration for the next issue.

Instituting the After-Conference Initiative

Of all the wonderful lessons learned at conferences, one that does not seem to sustain is change theory, as noted by the number of administrators who push the post-conference idea.

Now please do not misunderstand the message. Conferences are wonderful learning experiences, and many tremendous ideas have been discovered both in the planned sessions and among the less formal conversations at said events. However, nothing tells a staff "you are not doing it right" than spending a day or two with the next guru and returning to Dodge with a host of new proposals that will "really change" what we are doing here.

Noticeably, change can be good, and maybe your school does need a jumpstart, but to marry new initiatives with outside ideas undermines the greatness that lies within. In other words, one might be better served building the capacity for said idea than to just drop it on the staff like an aerial assault.

Remember the meeting before the meeting? Preparation for change is just as critical as the change itself if we desire an effective implementation and a sustained approach for success. Those that dartboard the next lifesaver as a method of leadership usually wind up with holes in their plans.

Patience is the key. Move too slowly, and everyone is past you; move too quickly, and all are behind.

NOTE

1. A. Barber, *The Hidden Principalship: A Practical Guide for New and Experienced Principals* (Lanham, MD: Rowman & Littlefield, 2013).

TWENTY-TWO

Case Studies

Case studies are situations that connect the topic to each chapter. They are designed to spur conversation and look to examine the key points of each chapter. Often, the case study is best when used prior to reading the chapter.

CHAPTER 1: JOINING THE DARK SIDE

Nicole believed that she was entitled to an explanation. Having turned in a referral to Thomas Hansen, the assistant principal at Whitmore Middle School, she was looking forward to discussing the issues. Unfortunately for her, the discussion was nothing more than a Post-it note in her mailbox stating, "I gave him two detentions."

As she discussed the situation with her colleagues, she was perplexed by Thomas's behavior. How could a guy who was just teaching with them two years ago be so unapproachable now? Maybe the whisper among the staff that Thomas was "one of them now" was starting to become a reality.

If you were Nicole, what would you do? Are teachers "entitled" to a decision concerning student discipline? If you did have the chance to speak with Thomas, what would you say? What is missing at this school? What does "one of them" mean?

Something to Consider

As administrators, we must find the time to provide rationale for our thoughts and decisions. To simply make decisions and assume trust based on our rank undermines collaborative communication. Plus, we need to see each situation as a chance for us to connect with our colleagues. Perhaps if we shared our thought process, we could start to build an appreciation for our value in the system.

CHAPTER 2: THAT'S WHY YOU MAKE THE BIG BUCKS

Krista Hynes was excited to be an administrative intern. She enjoyed her classwork, but really found satisfaction in her daily dealings with students and staff.

One day, while she was investigating a student situation, a fellow teacher, Brian, asked if she wanted to come watch the preview for the school play. Unfortunately, Krista had to decline because she was "right in the middle" of fixing the advisory schedule.

Brian, in a matter-of-fact tone, stated that it would not be long before Krista would "make the big bucks." Brian went to the play; Krista continued her inquiry.

If you were Krista, would you respond to Brian's tag? What is he trying to say to you? Do you agree? Is the topic really about money? What can we do about the perceived divide that exists between teachers and administrators?

Something to Consider

Although the literal meaning ties to financial gain, the hidden message speaks to power and a disconnection. Both Brian and Krista hold fault for not discussing the situation. Although Krista is currently working on a project, she is probably being perceived as placing a task (schedule) over a person (Brian's offer). Similarly, Brian's response does not truthfully correspond to his feelings. The "big bucks" represent the metaphorical separation between administrators and staff. And their acceptance of it is the damaging force to their relationship.

CHAPTER 3: THEY'RE INCOMPETENT!

Ted Houston was a caring, compassionate administrator who believed in the good of people. Regrettably, not everyone on Ted's staff felt as he did. Joan Causeway, a fourth grade specials teacher, believed that Ted was incompetent. Be it his dealings with students, parents, or staff members, no matter the decision, Joan believed Ted was on the wrong side of it. And she let everyone know.

On one occasion, another member of the staff challenged her thinking. He asked if Joan had ever been an administrator, alluding to the fact that she certainly judged him in a harsh manner without having a similar experience. Joan, almost instantly, retorted by stating, "If a tree falls in the forest and no one sees or hears it, does it mean that it did not fall?"

Her colleague left a bit perplexed.

Do you agree with Joan's belief system — can we judge incompetency for tasks we have never tried? What basis does Joan have for making her accusations? Does disagreement equate to ineffectiveness? How do you rank circumstances in your life? Is your competency based on these decisions? Should it be?

Something to Consider

Despite her apparent negative disposition, Joan embodies a popular belief in today's schools. Folks act like Monday-morning quarterbacks all the time. What we need to realize is that many folks agree on the end results, but few agree on the means to get there. This is the essence of consensus, and the crux for triage in systems of that sort.

CHAPTER 4: THEY'VE FORGOTTEN WHERE THEY ARE FROM: ONE MORE THING

Lucy Downs could not understand why her staff was so upset with her. Everyone knew the new social studies program was going to be implemented this fall. In fact, last spring the team spent three days with the representative from the company preparing for the implementation. Likewise, the summer sessions were well attended, and people really seemed content with the topics being covered.

With all of the prep work and countless discussions, why did so many staff members appear to be so upset? Finally, Lucy decided to ask a veteran colleague what was going on. He explained that folks were just feeling overwhelmed with "one more thing" to do. Lucy genuinely felt bad, but what more could she have done? The work needed to be accomplished. Right?

Can principals delegate work to staff members? Is this practice effective? How do teams address new initiatives? How would you? Did Lucy have a different recourse?

Something to Consider

Perhaps principals that have appeared to "forget where they are from" are really doing exactly what they did in the classroom, only now the audience has changed. Planning for change requires an effort and focus from all stakeholders. Those who plan in isolation, even to the greatest depth of detail, ultimately miss key factors in the process of building a shared vision.

CHAPTER 5: WHAT DO THEY DO UP THERE ALL DAY?

Have you ever been driving, saw a person speeding, and thought to yourself, "Where are the police when you need them?" Regina Flowers was such a person. She was really good at finding situations that required the administration's attention; however, she was even better at complaining how the principals "were never there when you needed them."

Thinking back to the police example, what do you think causes this phenomenon? Compare it to that of the principal's situations. In assuming good intentions, do we really believe administrators do not want to administer? As teachers, what can we do about this situation?

Something to Consider

The old saying "out of sight, out of mind" holds weight in this instance. Sometimes it is easy for us to assume people are not working when they do not have a specific task to attend. In addition, when placed into situations where we do not hold the ultimate power (person to police, teacher to principal), we can sometimes get discouraged by not having the ability to correct it. We must work to understand that we do not know everything that occurs in a system, and we must try to become educated in different aspects of it to build understanding and trust.

CHAPTER 6: LET'S MAKE A DEAL: THE PRINCIPAL

Claude Izzy was a business teacher in the Old South School District. Claude was a no-nonsense guy and had little time for foolishness. When Claude had student issues, he usually handled them on his own. Unfortunately, his dealings with Timmy needed office intervention.

To make a long story short, Claude saw Timmy as a disrespectful young lad and believed he needed to be suspended. On writing his first referral in five years, he was somewhat optimistic that Timmy would receive the appropriate consequence. He did not.

Dr. Miles, the assistant principal, did issue a detention to Timmy, but held off on the suspension. She did explain her rationale to Claude, but all that did was annoy him more. At lunch, he let the table know that he would not be writing another referral again because he had learned his lesson. "Dr. Miles wants to make deals and be friends."

Is Claude justified in his thought process? Should principals suspend students based on recommendations from the staff? Should an adult's testimony trump an investigation? How would you respond to this question: "Why do we have a discipline book if we are not going to follow it?"

Something to Consider

Is it easy to get into a car traveling at 100 miles per hour? If not, why do teachers become so angry at principals for not being as upset regarding a discipline situation that they are just entering? In other words, we must afford administrators the right to process the situation and balance it according to what is best for the child. We may not agree on the outcome, but once we turn in a referral, we forego the right to control its result.

CHAPTER 7: SHE HAS HER FAVORITES

Mindy Stevenson was a fantastic teacher and teammate, but truth be told, she was not pleased with the way that her current team leader was performing. Mindy was not obsessed with being a team leader, but she did think about the possibility whenever issues arose. She truly believed she would give more effort than the current one, who did not care for the drama that came with new ideas.

When she would approach the subject with her closest friends in the building, they would all caution her about their principal, Mr. Douglas, and his relationship with the current team leader; they were friends outside of school. In fact, their families even vacationed together. Mindy would always become discouraged when the discussion got to this point. And as usual, she would dismiss the idea and sit a bit lower during the next team meeting.

If you were Mindy, what would you do? What is within your power? Is it okay for the boss to have favorites? If the boss truly has favorites, what can be done?

Something to Consider

To think that administrators do not have favorites is foolish. However, this does not mean that these people should be awarded special treatment. If you want to lead, you have every right to seek opportunities to do so. Volunteer for different activities, clubs, or other events outside the classroom. Find your passion and look to secure its place in your life.

Likewise, if folks are being shown a special fancy to the detriment of others, then by all means those issues should be addressed as well.

CHAPTER 8: THIS TOO SHALL PASS

Micah Jacobs was a conscientious science teacher who did his best to follow the guidelines for lab safety. Lately though, his patience was waning. Dr. Stubbs, the science coordinator, had just instituted new safety regulations for labs that would force teachers to perform a tremendous amount of prep work prior to the lab even starting. Without any additional prep time, the teachers were skeptical about how they would be able to accomplish such tasks.

Additionally, Dr. Stubbs was a temporary replacement for the regular science supervisor, Martha Cobb, who was on maternity leave. Many folks believed she was unaware of Dr. Stubbs's changes, as he had a reputation of being a maverick.

If you were Micah, what would you do? Would you contact Martha? Would you follow the new regulations? Create a game plan and be sure to include the stakeholders?

Something to Consider

Certainly, safety is critical for our students and staff, and the efforts that go into the planning for lab safety are immense. However, administrators must be cognizant of making changes without considering different perspectives to the organization. Otherwise, these types of changes can be dismissed by teachers as "this too shall pass" initiatives.

Perhaps Micah can have a conversation with the principal. Maybe a clear explanation of what is expected and what the ramifications are to the system and people would assist everyone in attaining a better result. Supervisors who initiate change without the principal's knowledge are usually not successful.

CHAPTER 9: IT'S GOOD FOR KIDS

Dr. Ulrich was charged with raising the SAT scores. In realizing this task, he decided to institute an after-school session, whereby faculty members could volunteer to assist students in the process. Certainly, no one was expected to be an expert in the SAT. Dr. Ulrich hired two folks from a company to fulfill those roles. He was looking for teachers to be more of a support for the process and on standby when a student needed extra support.

Buddy Meeks was a high school teacher who also played music on the side. Unfortunately, the SAT sessions were held on Tuesdays and Thursdays, the same days as his band obligations. Therefore, Buddy was unable to volunteer.

A few weeks into the program, Dr. Ulrich noticed that Buddy was not assisting his colleagues. He decided to have a conversation with him. During the conversation, Dr. Ulrich told Buddy that these sessions were "good for students" and also mentioned that his colleagues seemed to have their "priorities" in the right place.

If you were Buddy, how would you respond to this discussion? Can someone judge our outside activity as detrimental to the organization? If so, where is the line drawn on such judgments? As a principal, is this line of "support" for students sustainable?

Something to Consider

Many initiatives would be good for students if we could afford and staff them (individual tutoring, laptops for everyone, etc.). Administrators that pressure teachers to perform tasks under this belief system create a dreadful working environment. We must look to build other motivators in addition to support for students.

CHAPTER 10: SHE BEATS THE KIDS TO THE BUSES

Principal Yolanda Givings is really upset with Chase Mason. When she requested that Chase assist with the after-school homework club, Chase politely refused, as he needed to attend to "other critical events" in his life.

However, Yolanda was not buying it. She knew that Chase played on an adult softball team and that he participated in a host of other activities. However, instead of addressing her concerns with him, she simply labeled him as a slacker and treated him as such. Chase was unaware of Yolanda's feelings toward him, but always wondered why he was never selected for any school or district-level committee or leadership team.

Is Chase justified in saying no to Yolanda's request? If you were Yolanda, what would you do? Is this a contract issue?

Something to Consider

There are many folks in the organization who cannot perform certain tasks, but could be really assets in other areas. Too often, we allow one instance or event to taint the next one. By avoiding the dialogue, the separation increases between Yolanda and Chase, even without his knowledge.

Additionally, if Yolanda believed Chase lied to her (which I am not sure that he did with the words he selected), she probably should chat with him about it instead of allowing the annoyance to fester. She cannot force him to do anything after school, but developing a trusting relationship is not grounds for a grievance.

CHAPTER 11: GETTING THE BUY-IN: DRINKING THE KOOL-AID

Owen Ross, a special education teacher in Claire Ville, was at his wits end. In being directed that every change to an IEP had to be completed through a meeting, he was beside himself wondering how he would accomplish this task and still teach his classes. In fact, even the slightest of tweaks now required a meeting, when in the past, a phone call would have sufficed.

Owen was concerned with following the legal guidelines and was not one for causing a ruckus, but something had to change.

If you were Owen, please plan out your strategy on how you would handle this situation. If you were Owen's administrator, what support could you offer him? Is there ever a time when we can forgo following every legal mandate?

Something to Consider

In a perfect world, certainly, we would want to afford each family with a personal meeting every time an event was directly related to their student. Nonetheless, this type of personalization at a micro level seems unmanageable.

Obviously, the current administration did not alleviate Owen's stress level when the change was originated. Yet it is incumbent on the team to look at every aspect of the job and prioritize what can and cannot be accomplished. Otherwise, folks will start to cut out individual pieces based on personal judgments.

CHAPTER 12: YOU WORK FOR A DISTRICT, NOT A SCHOOL

Becky Thurman was just hired as the new human resource director in her school district. She believed that teacher transfers should be communicated to the staff by the principals, as they were the ones making the decisions at the staffing meetings, and could answer more direct questions pertaining to the change. Plus, she believed the principals could make the discussion more personal (less dramatic, more caring) because they really knew the individuals.

Despite her position, the principals were not as apt to have these discussions, as they believed the HR person's responsibility was to direct staffing. Likewise, since the district had always had the HR person deliver this message, they were not in agreement that tradition needed to be broken. Actually, some principals believed Becky just did not want to be the bad person in this situation.

What is your opinion on this issue? If transfers are necessary, who should deliver the news? What type of a system would support the district and the teacher?

Something to Consider

In districts that perform transfers, the process for distributing the news can make or break the morale of the staff. Every effort must be made to be as honest as possible so that we do not create mistrust. Simply sending someone to another school without some sort of explanation damages the relationship. Perhaps this should be a combined effort.

CHAPTER 13: SHE HAS NO WALLS

Patty Deben, a reading specialist at Lions Middle School, was very knowledgeable about literacy and loved to share it. Unfortunately, her desire to share was more than a little overbearing for the staff at Lions. In fact, she was a literacy junky.

Staff members appreciated Patty's knowledge, but simply could not stand her approach. Quite simply, she was constantly talking. Whether in the faculty room, mail room, or lunch room, Patty was desperate to grab someone's ear and unload on her latest article or finding. Never as a mean practice, she would even interrupt presenters at literacy meetings to share her thoughts.

If you were on staff with Patty, what would you do? How would you approach a conversation with her without starting a fight or crushing her confidence? If you were the principal, would you have an obligation to address this situation? How would you handle it?

Something to Consider

Folks that talk and talk and talk do cause stress to their colleagues. Whether Patty is lonely or just loves to hear her own voice, the means do not justify the end result of taxing the staff's patience. Principals do need to address this situation, as failure to do so will start to impact the feel toward literacy (in-services, discussions, etc.).

A principal used to film her in-service days to archive them for future needs. With a similar situation, she asked a constant talker to watch the tape to see if she noticed anything. The practice worked, as the person returned the tape and let her know she would try to curb her enthusiasm.

CHAPTER 14: THE BUCK STOPS HERE! NO SURPRISES

There are times in schools when events that occur within our realm of control will exit and proceed on to the next level. In those cases, our boss would probably be better served having a heads-up on the topic rather than being surprised by an unsolicited meeting or phone call.

In realizing that we can never predict every occurrence, can you list events or situations where you believe the principal needs to have a heads-up? Try to categorize them. If you were the principal, would your list be similar?

Something to Consider

We are all in this together, and the sooner we can understand each other's vantage point, the better we will be at communicating and connecting. Again, 100 percent certainty does not exist; however, even the initial discussion will build empathy and openness. See the possibilities and build the team through critical conversations.

CHAPTER 15: THROWN UNDER THE BUS!

Margaret Paterson did not mean to tattle on her principal, Dr. Bob. Superintendent Woodward was attending a basketball game at Margaret's school. As they were conversing, Dr. Woodward asked where Dr. Bob was. Margaret, without even thinking, told him that Dr. Bob has child care issues and rarely attends after-school sporting events.

Two days later, Dr. Woodward had a meeting with Dr. Bob, and since Dr. Bob told his secretary, everyone in the school knew the situation and came to the conclusion that Margaret had thrown Dr. Bob under the bus.

If you were Margaret, what would you do? Do you need to do anything? Were there any initial steps that could have occurred? Should Dr. Bob chat with Margaret? Does he have a right to that conversation?

Something to Consider

If these two people do not have a conversation, their relationship will certainly take an enormous hit. Understanding intent is critical in these situations, especially if they want to salvage the affiliation.

However, perhaps Margaret knew what she was saying. Maybe she did want the superintendent to know about Dr. Bob's quick exits. Who knows? In this situation, the relationship is already damaged. Yet this is even more of a reason to talk to see if it can be repaired.

CHAPTER 16: I DO IT FOR THE KIDS

Bud, a third grade reading teacher, was a man of conviction and self-righteousness. He operated in a genuine spirit for the interests of the kids, as demonstrated by his tag line: "I do it for the kids. They are the only ones I care about."

Sarah, a team member of Bud's, was sometimes at the focal point of Bud's assertions. Although respectful, Sarah did not always agree with Bud's tactics. In response to her perceived dissention, Bud would retort with his usual clip about being the "only one" who has the best interests of the kids in mind.

If you were Sarah, would you say anything? If so, what would it be? Would you go to the principal? What if you were the principal? Would you address his behavior? How would you stay positive?

Something to Consider

Even if Bud is the most polite, well-mannered man on the face of the earth, we must take the time to educate him on how he is making the team feel. Those who position the students to justify their beliefs misuse them. We all do for the students. How we do (what our beliefs are) varies, which causes the need to negotiate.

When we substitute the needed discussion with a slogan, we separate ourselves from not only the issue at hand, but our colleagues as well.

CHAPTER 17: IT IS WHAT IT IS

Teresa Flynn, a technology teacher at Alcove Elementary School, had been here before. For seven months, the technology team (which she was the leader) had been discussing whether to use laptops or tablets. As the team was close to reaching a decision, the technology director for central office told them that the school board decided to go with tablets and that the committee was no longer needed on this project.

On hearing the news, Teresa replied, "It is what it is; yet, if you would have waited two days, the team was about to select the tablets."

Have you ever been involved with a situation like this one? Describe it. How did you feel? Do you still harbor feelings for this situation? Does Teresa hold any power in this situation? How would you handle this circumstance? What would you tell your team?

Right off the bat, we cannot lie about the decision. The worst thing would be to tell the team they made the decision when the board already did. Inevitably, someone will find out and Teresa will lose her credibility. Honesty, although difficult, would be the best approach.

Teresa's power lies within her feelings. How we deal with situations defines our character. Just because this occurrence was faulted does not mean the next one will be.

CHAPTER 18: ALL I DO FOR THIS PLACE

Lenny Harley was an art teacher at Haven Woods High School. Every year, Haven would host an art exhibit. What started off as a showing of a few pieces after school had grown to a full evening event. The Haven Art Gala was now sponsored and actually raised over $7,500 for the school. It was an enormous community event, and people from as far as three towns over would come to see the magnificent work being accomplished at Haven.

Although Lenny was the one linked to its success, this year he was really bitter. Talk on the school board was to modify the art curriculum course offerings. Although this would not impact the gala, the changes could possibly alter a few of Lenny's day classes.

On hearing the news, Lenny was furious. He believed he should have been consulted on the topic because art would not even be a topic if it were not for him and the gala. He even went on to say that if these changes were made, he would stop sponsoring the gala.

Does Lenny have the right to be upset? If you were him, what would you do? What happens to people who do for themselves? Do you think the gala would go on without him?

Something to Consider

Those who perform the work for the glory usually end their careers lonely and angry. Accolades can be most found in the spirit of doing a job because we know it needs to be done. Looking for the pat on the back keeps us focused on what is behind us instead of what is in front.

CHAPTER 19: THE DANCE OF THE LEMONS

Robin Mercy was touring her new building. She had just been transferred to Perce Middle School, and she was anxious to meet the staff and students. Having spent several years in her former building, she was excited for the opportunity to reinvent herself.

However, during the tour, she got the feeling that the other staff members were a bit leery of her. She even believed she heard someone say, "That's the one they wanted out."

If you were Robin, would you address this comment? Would you chat with the principal? Why would someone even make this type of comment in the first place? Is Robin's reputation already in question? How can we combat this type of situation?

Something to Consider

Regrettably, there are those who judge a person being transferred as an underachiever at his or her current building. There are various reasons folks receive a transfer; we must strive to withhold judgment and allow that person a chance to be successful.

In addition, in systems where the deadwood (ineffective staff members) is moved along instead of addressed, we create the feeling of despair by informally telling the staff it is okay not to do one's job well. We must hold ourselves and our staff accountable for the highest achievement possible. We can start by not allowing poor professionals to continue to be ineffective.

V

Questions from the Field

TWENTY-THREE

Questions from Teachers

1. THE TRANSFER

"I have been in my building for thirteen years. It has been great, but I am really in need of a change. I am thinking about putting in for a transfer, but I do not want my current colleagues to think I am deserting them. Any thoughts?"

A Possible Solution

Chat with your principal. Explain the situation. The last thing you want is for him or her to notice your name on a transfer list without knowing the reasoning behind the decision. Your principal might be able to assist if your desires are known. Likewise, if you happen to get the transfer, it is best just to tell your colleagues the truth. If someone is upset because you are following your passion, then she probably was not a true colleague in the first place.

2. INAPPROPRIATE REMARKS

"My principal loves to try to be funny, but I really feel like his sense of humor is over the line. What should I do?"

A Possible Solution

Hopefully, by reading this text, you both will have a more open relationship so that you would be able to tell him or her how you feel. However, if you are not there yet, you always can chat with the union or even someone above the principal. Just be sure to have specifics. Generalizations do not generate sustainable action. And please, do not send the

145

anonymous note. Anonymous notes are terrorist acts by folks who hide in the shadows. Own your beliefs. Limit the conspiracies.

3. NO EMOTION

"My principal always asks us to be passionate people when dealing with our students and families, and yet she barely bats an eye when discussing the goings on of our building. It is like do as I say but not as I do. Is there anything that can be done in this situation? I really want her to show excitement about what we do!"

A Possible Solution

This is not an uncommon request. Teachers are asked to be the lightning rods of the buildings and when the principal is deadpan, it has the potential to bring others down. However, it is very difficult to change someone's personality, especially if she has been successful (ascended to this point) in her career. Try to look for opportunities to acknowledge when she is passionate about something. These types of positive pats can go a long way. Nonetheless, whether she changes or not, you must continue to stay positive. No one can make you feel a certain way unless you agree to it.

4. LEADERSHIP

"I really would like to assume more of a leadership role in my building, but I have only been there for two years. Is it appropriate for me to do so? I feel like some of the more seasoned teachers may be upset with me."

A Possible Solution

Leadership is not dictated by age or experience. Of course, if you were brand new you might want to acquire the lay of the land before you look to establish yourself. (Leaders listen more than they talk, especially in the beginning.) Let your principal know. Volunteer for different events and do your best to remain positive. In other words, lead for the right reasons and all will be fine.

5. TAXING THE BUSY

"My principal is constantly asking me to direct professional-development sessions. Even though I do enjoy leading these events, it is becoming overwhelming,

as some of my other duties suffer during these times. Plus, I am starting to feel like he is taking advantage of my passion for professional practice."

A Possible Solution

Again, an honest conversation would be the best approach here. Certainly, you do not have to give up planning altogether. Maybe there is a way to split the effort with another person. Now if the initial conversation goes awry or you simply cannot have a conversation about this situation, I would suggest chatting with a union person for support. Unless this type of activity falls under your jurisdiction (a coach or staff developer), you need to truly be focused on your primary function as a teacher.

6. FEEDBACK

"My colleagues tell me I am in the minority, but when my principal or central office person visits my room, I want feedback. How can I ever improve if I do not receive timely feedback? The 'all is well' walkthrough is simply not cutting it."

A Possible Solution

You are not in the minority. Most folks, if observed, would want to receive some type of information concerning their performance. The simple "you are doing a great job" is polite but does not lend itself to continuous improvement. Maybe you could take an offensive approach and invite someone in with the intent of giving you feedback. Ask them to focus on a specific area at first. Take the initiative.

7. DELAYED SCHEDULE

"Every time we run a two-hour delayed schedule, I lose ten minutes of my planning period. I do not want to seem like a nitpicker, but ten minutes really adds up when you are busy. What would you do?"

A Possible Solution

Perhaps you could make an appointment with the person who works on the schedule. Obviously, you are not looking to ignite a confrontation; however, maybe the person is unaware of this situation. Certainly, if they are aware of it and still insist that it is warranted (against a contract), you would have the right to pursue its adjustment. However, try the "more bees with honey" approach first.

8. EXPECTATIONS IN MEETINGS

"Every time we have a parent meeting and it runs past the end of the workday, my principal states that this work is 'part of our professional responsibility' to stay without compensation. Is it?"

A Possible Solution

That answer depends on your contract. You need to check it out to see what it says about professional meeting times. However, even though the principal believes this to be true, the contract will define the accepted response. If there is not contract language, perhaps a conversation about the reasons you cannot stay (child care, commitments) is needed. Likewise, those who harbor ill feelings without expressing them sometimes develop a tendency to be negative. The sooner you can rectify the situation (and your feelings), the better for all.

TWENTY-FOUR

Questions from Administrators

1. UNION DILEMMA

"The union is constantly on me for little items. Whenever an issue comes up, I have to meet with the union leadership instead of the person with the issue. Is this some type of tactic unions use to gain power?"

A Possible Solution

My gut tells me that there is a greater issue occurring than the ones that are coming to you. Unfortunately, if folks feel that they need to go to the union every time there is a problem, then the problem may be a trust issue with the office or some other administrative rank. I would try to meet with the union representatives and see what is going on. If you are new, maybe this is the way things had to be handled in the past. You won't know until you ask.

2. SOCIAL EVENTS

"My staff is awesome! I feel so fortunate to be with them, but I have a problem. I am always invited to go to social events (parties) with them, but I decline because I do not want to infringe on their fun. Is this wrong?"

A Possible Solution

Is this wrong? No. There is no wrong answer here. Some folks attend the function for a little while and then leave early. This does not mean that you do not want to enjoy their company, but that you respect their need to "blow off steam" without their boss watching. Remember, you are still the principal. Now, if you decide to go and stay the entire time, that is possible as well. It depends. No definite answers here.

3. MY FAMILY NEEDS

"As the principal, I attend every social event in the school. I want to support our staff and students in their passions, but lately I am starting to feel like I am missing my family. I have a newborn and an older daughter, and she is starting to ask, 'Where's Daddy?' when I am not around. Any suggestions would be appreciated."

A Possible Solution

Such is the life of a building administrator. Perhaps you can start bringing your daughter with you to the events. This may give the person that is watching your newborn a break and also could be a great opportunity to bond with your daughter. If that is not possible, maybe there are some events that can be covered by another person. Ultimately, a building administrator has nights and weekends. That is just part of the deal.

4. GIVE ME FIVE

"Is it wrong for me to feel that certain teachers are 'playing me' when it comes to time? For example, I ask a person to cover five minutes extra for a duty, and this guy is putting in a time card to be paid. For five minutes! This is the same guy that I allow to leave early when he has a doctor's appointment. Am I wrong for being upset with this situation?"

A Possible Solution

Heck no! But certainly you do not want to get into a tit for tat debate with him or other members of the staff. Talk to him. Explain how you feel. But do not hold the permission to leave early for the doctor's over his head. That is just not a morale card you want to play. I am pretty sure once you explain yourself, he will get the point. Now, if he does not, then I might chat with a union representative for a little added support.

5. MY BOSS IS A MICRO-MANAGER

"My assistant superintendent is a micro-manager, and it is driving me crazy! I have been in this position for seven years, and I know what I am doing. This guy has been here for a year and a half, and he is constantly infringing on my power as the principal of the building. What can I do to survive this?"

A Possible Solution

That is a difficult situation to be in. My first thought would be to solicit some feedback from him. Is there something specific concerning him? In being new, maybe he is trying to educate himself on the culture of the buildings. Or perhaps he does not know what to do as a central office person and is just doing what comes naturally (being a principal) until he secures his footing. (I was definitely guilty of this in the beginning.) The answers reside in the conversation. However, if you cannot take it, and your boss is not going anywhere, you may have to think big picture.

6. LIVE IN THE DISTRICT

"I live in the district where I am an administrator. I have been in the district for many years, and for the most part, all has been well. However, this year the teachers are negotiating a contract with the board and it is not going as planned. People are very angry and are starting to pick sides. I am starting to feel a bit trapped."

A Possible Solution

That's understandable. There are pros and cons to living in the same district where you work. Do your best to stay neutral. Be empathetic and supportive of all parties. Remember, it is not your battle, so do your best not to enter the fray.

7. PREVIOUS PRINCIPAL IS IN CENTRAL NOW

"My boss was the principal of the building I am in now. I have not started the job yet, but am a bit worried about this situation. Any guidance would be valued."

A Possible Solution

It is only natural that your boss may have a bond with the staff or students in the building. This does not mean that she will be a thorn in your side. It really depends on her disposition. Ultimately, if she was part of the hiring process, she picked you to be the successor for a reason. My gut is telling me that in this situation, she would want you to succeed. Draw on her experiences; listen to her advice, but do as you see fit with the team.

8. TEACHER NOW PRINCIPAL

"I was a tenth grade science teacher in the building where I am now the new assistant principal. Although most folks have been really supportive, some are certainly treating me a bit oddly. How can I gain their trust in this new position?"

A Possible Solution

Do your job. It is that simple. If you do your job and keep people abreast of situations (proactive communicator), most people will value your inside experience and hopefully note that you have not "forgotten where you are from." Will you gather everyone into the fold? Nope. But this would be the case no matter who you are and where you were the principal. Do your job. Hold people to a positive standard and shine on.

VI

Looking Forward

TWENTY-FIVE

The Burden of Hope

The following is a letter from a father to his sons. Although it is not directly related to schools, it summarizes the intent of our journey and the commitment we must make to one another if we are ever going to build sustainable relationships.

If you learn nothing else; if all the days from this to that exhaust themselves into the awaiting abyss, always remember this last talk, my sons. Always remember this one.

There are those who wish to win the lottery every single day of the week and twice on the weekend, but you can only hope to win the lottery after you have purchased a ticket. The burden of hope manifests itself in the realization that it is only accepting the possibility of the loss that a true win can ever be attained. Much like myself for far too long, I would await the magic of possibly accomplishing the "great novel," which was nothing more than the sharing of ideas, the relays of our lives. However, in not starting the process, I had yielded the great nothing, leaving myself countless hours to wish and whine.

Both young and old have fathomed thought toward the existence of themselves in relation to simply being alive. In other words, among the pattern of comparison, we constantly search for the glimmering jewel outside of ourselves only to find it is ever-present within. As we have discussed previously, fear has a tendency to motivate us to the nonaction, and yet, despite knowing this in our very core, we struggle each day to find reason to continue amid the doubt and fury we call life. This, my sons, only leads us to the insanity of substituting calculated "filler" actions for fear of starting the one that burns deep in our hearts.

Loss, like any other experience, is a gift. Loss extends to us the possibility of anew. As the bare Dogwood awaits her pinkish hue, so too does loss provide us with the fertile ground for the next idea to grow. It is within the loss that the

155

*secrets of life most reveal themselves, for our focus is so keenly aware that we
exist despite our victories. I want for you to always cherish the losses. Sign up for
them and embrace the opportunity to be reborn. Though not an easy proposition,
it is one that I challenge you to take each day. You will find them in the moments
that await the moments you had anticipated. You will find them in the reflections
both of the past and of the future. You will find them.*

*It has taken a lifetime and a while to notice the patterns take shape. I do
believe that life gives us the same type of problem in various fashions until we are
able to recognize its presence. Yet, despite all of the possible variations within the
millions and millions of lighted brains, the simple solution to the puzzle was
always one piece away, one missed turn toward our destiny. I have loved like no
other; I have found goodness in the selfless acts of others, and have struggled to
climb the sheerest cliff found within my own spirit. And, at each, I have failed.
However, despite my mishaps, the melody still plays, especially when I close my
eyes and dream.*

*I find my hope in you, my sons. To be the man, you don't have to beat the
man; you just have to be, and believe. I believe in you. I believe in your ability to
take each of your wishes and mold them into lustrous hopes for your future and
the future of the human race. Hope sings within the human spirit. It is our
greatest sonnet, our truest chord.*

*In finality, I challenge you to purchase your ticket, my sons. Go after it; grab
it tight with both hands and never, ever let it go. Find yourself in your reflection
and the reflections of each other. And believe. Always believe.*

Love,
Dad

VII

Summation

Thank you for the purchase of this text. Hopefully, it will become a valuable resource in your educational library. Remember, whether we agree or not concerning the topics and strategies is not as critical as the conversations that sprout from our accord or disagreement. We must strive each and every day to have meaningful dialogue with one another. It is only through these critical connections that we will find true harmony.

Best of luck in your journey.
Tony

Bibliography

Barber, A. *The Hidden Principalship: A Practical Guide for New and Experienced Principals.* Lanham, MD: Rowman & Littlefield, 2013.

Barber, A., and J. Ulmer. *Common Threads: Investigating and Solving School Discipline.* Lanham, MD: Rowman & Littlefield, 2013.

Carnegie, Dale. *How to Win Friends and Influence People.* New York: Pocket Books, 1936.

Chomsky, Noam. *Cartesian Linguistics: A Chapter in the History of Rationalist Thought.* 3rd edition. New York: Cambridge University Press, 2009.

Clabaugh, K. G., and G. E. Rozycki. *Understanding Schools: The Foundations of Education.* New York: Harper & Row, 1990.

Dahl, Roald. *Charlie and the Chocolate Factory.* New York: Alfred A. Knopf, 1964.

Duckworth, A. L., C. Peterson, M. D. Matthews, and D. R. Kelly. "Grit: Perseverance and Passion for Long-Term Goals." *Journal of Personality and Social Psychology* 92, no. 6 (June 2007): 1087–1101.

Feinberg, W., and F. J. Soltis. *School and Society.* New York: Teachers College Press, 1998.

Hall, Edward T. *The Silent Language.* Greenwich, CT: Fawcett, 1959.

Johnson, Spencer. *Who Moved My Cheese?: An Amazing Way to Deal with Change in Your Work and in Your Life.* New York: Putnam, 1998.

Lucus, George. *Star Wars: Episode IV—A New Hope.* San Francisco: Lucasfilm, 1977.

Merriam, S. B. *Qualitative Research and Case Study Application in Education.* San Francisco: Jossey-Bass, 1998.

Scannella, Anthony. *Changing Student Behavior: Comprehensive Learning and Interventions for Correcting Kids.* Lanham, MD: Rowman & Littlefield, 2007.

Thomas, Dylan. *Do Not Go Gentle into That Good Night.* New York: Richard Reynolds & John Stone, 1951.

Thurber, James. *The Secret Life of Walter Mitty. The New Yorker.* NY, 1939.

Zelinsky, Paul. *The Wheels on the Bus.* New York: Penguin, 1990.

CPSIA information can be obtained at www.ICGtesting.com
Printed in the USA
BVOW01s0301100614

355832BV00001B/7/P